BETWEEN THE POLES
'Creative living between atheism and religion'

CHRISTOPHER S SCOTT

BETWEEN THE POLES
'Creative living between atheism and religion'

BY

CHRISTOPHER S SCOTT

NEW MILLENNIUM
292 Kennington Road, London SE11 4LD.

First published September 1996
Reprinted December 1996

Printed and bound by Morgan Technical Books Ltd.
Wotton-under-Edge, Gloucestershire
Issued by New Millennium*
ISBN 1 85845 078 0
*An imprint of The Professional Authors' & Publishers' Association

To
Ruth

ACKNOWLEDGEMENTS

All quotations from the Bible are taken from The New Oxford Bible, New Revised Standard Version 1991. Other quotations used are acknowledged within the text or referenced.

There are many people who have played a part in the writing and publication of this book, too many to name in full. But there are three in particular, who laboured over my dyslexic manuscripts in order to make them readable, Mary Gueritz, Jenny Zarek and Sue Sabbagh who deserve special thanks. There are also the many people who have encouraged me to write, both through their personal support, and through the inspiration gained through reading their words. One person in particular has inspired me in recent times, Michael Nevin. For his support and humorous teaching of theology, I shall always be grateful.

CONTENTS

FOREWORD

When I was a student for the ministry, I noticed that the advice my teacher gave from the pulpit could be very different from the advice he gave in his private office. When I protested (being a self righteous prig), he said 'In the pulpit you must preach public truths, traditional truths. But in your office regard each situation as an exeption.'

I thought that was great advice, very sophisticated, very compassionate. But the more I pondered it, the more uneasy I became. It led to situations in which one thing was said from the pulpit, and another whispered in private. So religion and reality drifted apart from each other until the former became false to itself. Religion spent so much time on higher truths, it didn't bother enough about common honesty. Too much role playing was required.

I was immediately attracted to this book, because it is not just about the Higher Truths, but it is also personal and honest about the author's own life experience and spirituality and his interpretation of them in human terms. It's the real McCoy!

He has to find personal words to communicate his personal truth, like 'cojective'. But I understand easily because the experience he describes is shared by all seekers.

Now my own search has led me a different way - to what I term divine rather than human. But then I am approaching those truths from a different direction with my own special needs. It is placing the 'scriptures' of other people's lives alongside one's own that the depths and heights and awesomeness of the truth, which embraces us all, begins to appear. But first we have to be faithful to our own place in the puzzle.

This book is faithful. It is a private scripture, and I am grateful to Chris Scott for letting us share it.

Rabbi Lionel Blue

PART ONE

INTRODUCTION

It ain't necessarily so,
It ain't necessarily so.
The things that you're liable to read in the Bible,
It ain't necessarily so.

George & Ira Gershwin

These words voice the opinion of increasing numbers of men and women. While they recognise a spiritual dimension in their lives, they do not find their needs are met by institutional religion. The gap widens between the questions which people are asking, and the answers given by the Church. But the quest for meaning remains.

Not since John Robinson wrote *Honest to God* has the debate about the nature of religion been so alive. In 1994, Anthony Freeman became the first Church of England Priest for one hundred years to be sacked by his Bishop. His 'crime' was writing a book in which he tried to explore ways of understanding religious truths in a secular society. In fact, for trying to be honest to God.

I have written this book for people who know that the creeds, doctrines and scriptural interpretations of a bygone age will no longer do. In saying 'it ain't necessarily so,' I want to allow for alternative possibilities, rather than exchanging one set of rigid doctrines for another. This is a book for devout agnostics and fringe atheists. Those many thousands of people who sit uncomfortably at the edge of their religion, or beyond the edge, yet want to affirm that there is a meaning to life beyond the material.

I write with some trepidation, (not least because of Anthony Freeman's experience). As a one-time monk (Franciscan brother) and an ordained priest in the Church of England, my grounding is in the Christian faith. I know that I will be misunderstood by many

3

of my fellow Christians who read this book (and probably more still who will not read it!). Yet I feel compelled to write because I believe that the fundamental insights of all the great religions are primarily about being HUMAN, rather than being religious. The expression of religion must, by its very nature, narrow and confine thinking into manageable units. In the words of Parson Thwackum in Henry Fielding's 'Tom Jones' "When I mention religion I mean the Christian religion, and not only the Christian religion, but the Protestant religion; and not only the Protestant religion, but the Church of England." The line between constructing useful boundaries for purely practical reasons on one side, and bigotry and exclusiveness on the other, is a very fine one. Yet it is a line so often crossed. Not only does religion claim to have a monopoly on 'eternal values', but each different religion, and every sect and denomination within each religion claims its own particular brand of 'the truth'.

I want to affirm that naturally, human beings have what the Christian Church calls 'the Grace of God', and that it takes no supernatural intervention for people to live their lives to the full. Religion is not necessary to living a good and fulfilled life; to the contrary, it can be life denying and limiting, the very opposite of everything it proclaims to be true.

What I want to suggest is the possibility of a secular spirituality. This may sound like a contradiction in terms, but it is only so if one ties the concept of spirituality to a conventional religious belief system. In saying with Gershwin that 'It ain't necessarily so' I am wanting to let go of religious ideas that simply do not speak to women and men in the late 20th century. The very word 'God', which is central to most religions in its differing forms, is loaded with connotations which can, by the very nature of things, have little or nothing to do with the reality of which it purports to speak.

Secular spirituality is a way of being which may or may not

include religious thoughts and beliefs; neither its absence nor inclusion is a matter of importance. What is important is perception and attitude. Although the words spirit and spiritual are 'loaded' with religious connotation, I have retained them for two reasons. One is that I simply could not think of a better alternative (this book is going to be honest if nothing else), and the second is that it is quite possible to use the word spirit in a non-religious way. One might speak of the 'Spirit of England', or the 'Spirit of France', and who would want to deny that there is a difference in spirit between those two countries? Or the spirit of a particular game or sport such as rugby or cricket. Here we are talking about an ethos, a way of being that is not easily defined in prose, yet is somehow almost tangible to those who experience it. Experience plays a great part in spirituality. If someone were to talk to me about, say, the 'spirit of the mining community', I would have no first hand knowledge. I could not enter into the spirit, but would, rather, have second-hand perceptions from my somewhat limited knowledge of mining and miners.

Secular spirituality is concerned with affirming people where they are and in what they experience. In detail we all have very different lives, but we all have a shared humanity, a common beginning (even if it started in a test-tube) and a common end. In death we are all united.

As far as possible in writing this book I am going to avoid technical or professional language. Where I do use words which may not be familiar to a general readership, I shall endeavour to expand upon them within the text. This is done because I am aware of my own frustration when reading a non-technical book, which nevertheless uses words and phrases as though I had written a PhD on the subject. I suspect that I may call down the wrath of both theologians and psychologists alike for the way in which I handle material. But my intention here is not technical detail or contextual accuracy. The 'spirit' of this book is rather to make connections at a human and humane level, to say that beyond the technicalities and divisions of different disciplines lies the common ground of the Human Spirit. This is the essential part of our humanity which cannot be reduced to particular religious doctrines, or yield its nature to scientific or psychological analysis alone. If I appear to be cavalier with the material I use, it is because I have come to believe that the 'objective' nature of both science and religion can do as much to conceal the nature of the Human Spirit as it can to reveal it. Both can be valuable tools and should be treated with honesty and respect. But neither should be allowed to become a 'god', for in so doing, we diminish our true nature and live 'second-hand' lives.

If you have read thus far, you may have already decided that you are going to love this book, or hate it, ignore it or suspend judgement. Whatever you have decided will depend upon your perceptions, which leads us nicely into the first chapter...

CHAPTER 1
Seeing is Believing

Seeing, it is said, is believing. A few months ago I visited the Science Museum in London, (or was it the Natural History Museum?). One of the exhibits was a video recording of a street scene - a mugging I believe it was. I was then invited, via touch response on the video screen, to act as a witness. I was horrified to realise just how mistaken I was in my recollection. Had I been a real witness I would have testified against the wrong person. Yet it had been only minutes before when I had seen the event on screen, and I was expecting to be able to give an accurate account afterwards. What happened? Well, for one thing I know that I am not a very sensing person, that is, I will easily miss seeing, or at least noticing, what others will readily recall. But that is not the whole story. It would be good to think we see the world as it is, as an objective reality 'out there' - that our eyes and brains are just like a sophisticated camcorder, simply recording the world without distortion ready for instant and accurate play-back.

The truth is, as the philosopher Immanuel Kant said, "We see the world not as it is, but as we are." The studies of perception within psychology have shown us that we create reality rather than just observe it. Here is an example. I was looking through Crockford's clerical directory the other day when my eye alighted on this symbol.[1]

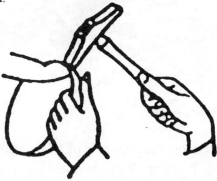

1. Illustration by Philip Hagreen

On looking at it, could you immediately tell what it is? I could not. I kept looking at it trying to 'see' what it was, but to no avail. I then looked at the accompanying text to see that it was advertising a silversmith. Once it was put in context, the meaning of the picture became clear; in fact on looking at it again whilst writing this chapter, I wonder how I could not have seen it. Because I have no knowledge of craft-work of any kind, I could not 'see' the meaning of the picture until it was put in context by further information. The visual image remained the same, and yet, within the space of moments the reality of it for me changed completely. By adding further information my perception changed and meaning was created.

Here is a more difficult example of the same sort of thing. Does the picture below mean anything to you? Or is it just a mass of blobs and spots?[2]

If I tell you that the picture is of a dalmatian in the snow, does that make it easier? Perhaps not. If it is driving you to

2. Richard Gregory, *The Intelligent Eye*, (1970)

distraction, go to the end of this chapter where it is made a little clearer. Once you have seen the dog, it is almost impossible not to see it. Our perception 'draws in' the outline to give meaning to an otherwise random collection of blobs on the page.

Many years ago, whilst doing a first-aid course, I heard the story of a girl who had had a serious cycling accident. She was lying unconscious and bleeding profusely from a wound in the groin. A man, who was a first-aider, was staunching the flow of blood by applying pressure to the femoral artery. A woman passer-by 'saw' what he was doing and also went to the girl's assistance. This she did by attacking the man with her umbrella! What she 'saw' was an accident victim being sexually assaulted. She had created her own reality from the visual stimulus of the situation, combined with her own experience and expectation.

Look at the figure below, what do you see?

Can you see the white triangle lying over three black circles? You can? - well done, you have just been creative. In reality there is no white triangle, your perception has created it from what your eyes have sensed, and from what you already know about shapes and angles. The triangle is a construction of our mind built upon previous experience. Ask a small child what he or she sees and they will describe only the partial black circles - or they may describe them in their own words via their own experience - so that the partial circle becomes a 'munching mouth' (like the Happy Eater sign). Such shapes as the one above have also been shown to adults of different cultures where angles and straight lines play little or no part in their lives, such as African Bushmen. Again, like the children, they will describe what they see in different terms, the triangle will not be apparent to them because it is not already part of their frame of reference.

My wife is something of a magician. Although she keeps most of her 'magic' a secret even from me, I have been let into some of the 'tricks of the trade'. She knows many tricks, and some of them she will not use because she feels that they are so obvious that anybody will immediately spot them. Of course she spots them when performed by others because of her knowledge. In this case her perception (that the trick is so obvious) prevents her from performing it herself and limits her repertoire. Her knowledge informs her perception, and her perception in turn affects her actions.

You may well be wondering why I have started this book with examples of perception, and the nature of perception as a creative process rather than just as a sense recording system. Yet I hope that by the time you have finished this chapter, I will have been able to make the point that truth and reality are not simply 'objects out there' onto which we have to focus, but that to a very great extent every individual creates his or her own truth and reality from a combination of external sensory data and internal experiential knowledge.

Given that no two individuals have exactly the same life

experiences, it follows that there is no such thing as absolute objective reality or truth unless it is a tautology, (To call a circle round is a tautology). In other words it is true to say that a circle is round - because that is the definition of a circle - but if it ceases to be round, it ceases to be a circle.

Apart then from definitions which are self-authenticating, we must realise that the reality of a situation as we perceive it will not necessarily be the same reality for another individual. We may be observing the same external object or event from the same physical perspective, and yet the creative activity of our perception is likely to give us a unique slant on what we term 'reality'. If this is so for the everyday world of material objects, events, encounters and transactions, how much more so must it be in the realm of the spiritual?

There may be some of you who, having read this chapter, will be thinking that I am being very subjective in my outlook. It may appear to the reader that what I am saying is that every individual decides for themselves the nature of what is true or real. This I believe is part of the truth, but only part. There is an interaction between people which, whilst in itself is not an objective and concrete reality 'out there', nevertheless forms the basis of our communication. Somewhere between the personal, unique and subjective, and the universal, common and objective lies the Spirit of Humanity.

It is my contention that true spirituality is concerned with this dimension of life which is common to all people. It is the area of interface between those disciplines which are often represented as opponents, for example, science and religion. In popular belief, science represents the totally objective, fact oriented view of life that disregards and eliminates (as if it could) any subjective material from its studies. Equally, religion is regarded as dealing with the 'other-worldly', as having a view of creation that often flies in the face of scientific knowledge, and that purports to speak objectively about a supernatural Being.

The dichotomy between science and religion is a false one. They are not talking about different realities, but about different perceptions of the same reality.

Let's look at an example. A couple go to a D.I.Y. store to look for a new front door for their house. They look at one and the man says "it's too heavy, that will not do". His wife on the other hand says "no it's just right, I'd really like to have that one". Both are convinced in their view and a long argument ensues. Who is right? Well as it turns out, both of them are. When the man says it is too heavy, he means literally, physically, it is too big and weighty and would require hinge mountings much stronger than their present door frame permits. His wife on the other hand is speaking metaphorically when she says it is just right, for she is referring, not to the literal weight and bulk, but to the tone and colour of the wood. He can be said to be representing the 'scientific' view, and she the 'religious', or to use less grand terms, the practical and the aesthetic respectively.

They are discussing the same reality but are encountering the problems of both perception and language. Each partner is concerned with different aspects of the one reality, i.e. the door, but because each has a preoccupation with their own particular concern at that moment, neither can hear what the other is saying. Both are 'telling the truth', but it is partial truth and not the whole truth. Here lies one of the greatest blocks to human fulfilment and happiness.

On every subject it is possible to have different views and opinions, both because of our own unique perceptions, and because we may be using quite different criteria when talking about the same reality. As a counsellor, I have spent a lot of time with couples whose relationships are 'on the rocks'. Time and time again one of the major problems is that of perception and perspective. Not only does each partner bring a unique perception to bear on a subject, but often each is simply focusing on different and limited aspects of the same reality. There will probably not be a single reader who has not experienced at first hand the destructive forces which can operate when 'lines have been crossed', (as in telephone lines, not demarcation lines), and communication has simply not been able to take place.

Some good friends of ours nearly came to grief in their relationship before it had properly begun. Both were working in America at the time and met there. Before one of them had to return to England, they arranged to meet up in one of New York's famous buildings, one with a bar on the top floor. Both knew the building, and each had a mental picture of where they should meet. Unfortunately neither was specific with the other. He spent a long time waiting in the top floor bar, whilst she was getting increasingly mad in the ground floor lobby. Having both arrived at the possibility that this might have happened, one ascended whilst the other descended in opposite lifts. By good fortune they did eventually coincide before it was too late.

It is the stuff of all good comedy and farce, and we laugh because we see ourselves there. But all too often it is not laughter but real pain that ensues from bad communication and different perceptions and perspectives. And the pain arises because we fail to appreciate the difference. So often we make the assumption that our reality is the same as everybody else's reality, and we become angry and upset, or feel rejected and afraid, when what is real for us, is denied by others

The polarisation of beliefs, views, perceptions and interpretations is what destructively divides humanity. In its lesser form it will cause minor upset and irritation; at its most extreme, it results in injury, death and international warfare. A spiritual way of life is, I believe, a way of living creatively 'between the poles'. It is where the split personality of the human race can become whole, because a spiritual view of life recognises in the heart of the other,

13

a reflection of the self, albeit very different. Unlike particular disciplines of religion or science which expect a conformity of view from its followers, the spiritual path expects no conformity and welcomes diversity. It discovers aspects of the truth in the most unlikely (to the individual) of places, and is open to the probability that 'my' truth is only partial, and may well need to change in the light of further exploration. The spiritual path is not for those who want certainty and security, but for those who wish to live their lives more creatively, where truth becomes an ever moving and expanding concept.

Chapter 2

Living between the poles

In the first chapter I spoke of the area between the subjective and the objective as the place where the spirit of humanity is found. It is a 'touching' place where mutuality and understanding are recognised. It is made known in shared experiences of love, beauty, tenderness, and empathy. It is where two or more people recognise in one another a unity of spirit. But before we go off down the path of happy clappy land, where all is brightness and light, we also need to be aware that this same spirit has its dark side. There is also a mutuality in hatred, violence, cruelty and greed. The human spirit of which I speak, the 'place between the poles', has both great creative and destructive potential. We may be united in great and truly humanitarian causes, but equally we may unite in evil and monstrous endeavours. The collective evil of the Nazi regime was an extreme example of what the dark side of the human spirit is capable of. Alas, we do not need to look only to history to see the result of this dark side of the human spirit. A glance in any daily newspaper or a viewing of the news programmes on television reveals only too clearly the demise of the human spirit.

Yet whilst acknowledging the power of the dark side of the human spirit for destruction, this book is about affirming the potential of the positive spirit within humanity, a spirit which transcends religions, beliefs, dogmas, creeds, scientific proofs, scepticism and polarity. For the sake of simplicity, and to eliminate as far as possible linguistic misunderstandings, when I use the term 'spiritual' or 'spirituality' from now on, I will be referring to the positive and life affirming nature of the human spirit and not to the destructive side.

The first thing we need to do is to try and make clear what I mean by the area between the subjective and the objective, this 'living between the poles'. In English there is no word for it. Not being a linguist I do not know if other cultures have a word to describe it; if there is, I am sure I will find out in due course. I shall try to define what I mean thus:

An area of experience which is at one level unique to the individual, inasmuch that it has no empirically provable reference point (subjective); Whilst at the same time this experience is held in common with others and appears to have an external source of its being (objective).

Or put more simply, an experience held in common is often perceived as having a source outside itself. And here is the sixty four-thousand dollar question. Is this experience real? Well certainly it is real for each of the individuals concerned, but is it more than a collective illusion? The experience that is common to all humanity (except perhaps for those individuals who have suffered great psychological or mental damage) is that of love. Love has no empirical basis, it cannot be proved in any scientific sense, yet those who share love with another know that it is real. And sometimes it is very obvious to those outside the relationship that love is a reality for them. Yet just what is it?

It is this area of common experience most easily understood through love that I am trying to get at. (Of course the dark side as expressed in hate is equally real to those who experience it). It is neither completely subjective, that is, unique to one individual, nor is it objective, an 'out there fact' for all to see. It is between the two, almost impossible to express (you can see how I am struggling), and yet it is common to all humanity. It is I believe the very spirit of what it means to be human.

Humanity is often defined in rather concrete terms, the ability to reason and think, to communicate in both written and spoken languages, and to be able to transcend time by the process of memory and imagination. These are all things which, to a large degree can be measured and tested. Yet whilst all these things are true, there is surely also this 'fifth dimension' of spiritual integration which most people 'feel in their bones' as a reality, even if they are unable to put a name to it, or if it goes against the grain of their scientific view point.

This meeting point between the poles has of course not gone unrecognised before; it is simply that particular groups have claimed it as their own. It might be called the 'soul' or the 'spirit of God', or the 'psyche'. The problem with this is that each group starts with its own perceptions and goes on to describe this human phenomenon in a language common to itself, but alienating to those who do not share the same starting point. In naming or describing this centre point, the centre has automatically been put out of balance and drawn to one pole or the other. Either a religious connotation will be attached, with all the 'baggage' of that particular religion, or scientific explanations will be made which deny the experience of millions of people. We struggle therefore with perceptions, language and definition, not of different realities, but of the same reality understood differently. The attempt to understand and communicate the very essence of our human nature becomes yet another tool for causing a split.

This phenomenon which is common to human experience, and lies between subjectivity and objectivity I am going to call cojectivity. If individuals and groups are willing to suspend their exclusive claims for people other than themselves, then cojectivity can become the meeting place where peoples of different religious understandings or none, can come together in a common understanding of their humanity. This does not mean that a Christian needs to deny his belief, or that a Buddhist needs to change her path, or that an agnostic has to turn believer. In cojectivity all can recognise that there is a common human spirit, and therefore a spiritual path, but that each person will, through their own perceptions, choose a particular way to express it. This opens up a way, not only for more respect and tolerance between different faith groups, but for those who wish to express the essentially

17

spiritual nature of their being in secular or humanistic terms.

Cojectivity is the recognition that as human beings we have a potential for creative and positive living which is not limited to individuals. Neither is it the property of particular faith or interest groups, but is the essence of our humanity which is known and recognised in its shared and common nature. Cojectivity is the touching place I spoke of earlier, where humanity meets humanity beyond the systems and parameters that we build for ourselves. It is a point where the individual breaks the bonds of his or her individual perception to see a vision of what is possible.

This chapter feels as though it has been a bit heavy, so let me lighten it with a story.

Some years ago, when I was a curate (assistant priest) in a Shropshire town, my wife had some visitors whilst I was out. These visitors were two women, probably in their early thirties, and members of the Jehovah's Witnesses. Ruth invited them in, and what followed was a long discussion about the nature of the Bible, belief, faith and the 'life to come'. When I returned home, their conversation had been in progress for well over an hour, but neither Ruth nor our visitors were any nearer in seeing one another's points of view. I then joined in the rhetoric (for that is what it was, neither was really listening to the other), and on we went for a further period of time.

As the morning wore on, Ruth excused herself to go into the kitchen to get on with some clearing up left over from breakfast which I had not been able to finish. One of the two women went out into the kitchen to join her. She picked up a tea towel and started helping with the chores. Talk of theology and religion stopped and they began to speak about more personal things.

At that time, Ruth was working as a counsellor in a doctors' practice, and had not long before qualified as a midwife. As the conversation progressed, our visitor revealed that recently, she had suffered the stillbirth of her baby and was still in the process of grieving the loss. From Ruth's experience of having suffered a miscarriage, and from her training in midwifery and counselling, heart met heart. All the arguments of the previous hours about doctrine and belief seemed as irrelevant as yesterday's weather forecast. What had been happening in the long discussion was that each person's subjective belief was being presented as an objective truth. Now, in the meeting of pain and understanding, the shedding of tears, and the letting go of barriers, the human spirit of each person was able to meet, and to recognise and love the other. This is cojectivity. This is that universally experienced moment when we can move beyond the confines of our own limited experience, yet at the same time, we are not in the realms of material facts or empirical proofs.

The most profound and meaningful moments of our lives are cojective. They are experiences which are held in common with other human beings, although often they can only be communicated by means of poetry, song, art, music, myth or symbol. Sometimes the cojective experience is most powerfully recognised, not in any form of external communication, but in silence. Moments of love, joy, grief or sorrow are felt directly - heart to heart - they are known to be real, to be the most important occurrences in people's lives, yet they do not constitute anything which could be called objective or factual.

This hinterland of cojectivity which we all experience, yet which seems to defy our attempts to express in language without being objectified, is the essence of humanity, and the subject of this book. It is the most real thing in the world, yet of itself and on its own, it does not exist. It is the go-between which unites human existence and gives it the potential for both divine-like goodness, and demonic badness.

The wonderful little story by Margery Williams called 'The Velveteen Rabbit' illustrates the cojective at work.

'What is REAL' asked the rabbit one day... 'does it mean

19

having things that buzz inside you and a stick-out handle?'

'Real isn't how you are made,' said the Skin Horse. 'It's a thing that happens to you. When a child loves you for a long, long time, not just to play with, but REALLY loves you, then you become Real.'

Like all great fairy stories, the Velveteen Rabbit is telling your story and mine. 'Real' is not to be found in the objective, 'things that buzz and have stick-out handles', nor in the subjective, 'just being played with', but with the interaction between human beings. We are most 'real' when we are living 'between the poles'. It is a grey area full of risk and potential, danger and fulfilment. It is where the Human Spirit dwells and flows and meets, and it goes by many names.

CHAPTER 3
What's in a name?

When our daughter Freya was five years old. like all children of that age, one of her most frequent questions was 'Why?'. As any parent will know, it is a joy to have a child who is full of interest, but sometimes the response to constant 'why's' become hard to sustain. Recently, when we have been telling Freya the name of different things, her response has been "why is it called that?". Sometimes it is easy to answer, but often we have to respond with simply "well that's just what it's called."

Giving something or someone a name is a shorthand way of being able to hold a conversation. Imagine the following statement used without names, but using description instead. 'I placed my cup and saucer containing tea on to the table'. Let's make a start on what it might be like. 'I placed my container, which was round at the top, about three inches across and tapering to one inch across at the bottom, the taper being uneven with the full width extending to two thirds down the length. It had a protrusion on the side of a hollow semi-circular nature which allows for holding when the container is full of hot liquid. The basic colour was white with an intricate design...' I am sure you get the picture.

Without names to give a short-hand to our conversations, conversations would become impossible. Or at least, we would have huge detail about very limited areas. We use names, but in doing so we are assuming a great deal about the other person's knowledge of the subject matter, and implicitly we are saying that the detail is left to the listener to fill in. In everyday matters, like the conversation about the teacup and saucer, detail is usually completely irrelevant and does not detract from the general understanding and communication.

However, even for common place names important mistakes

can happen. One is that there might be two things with the same name. Some years ago I used to help out at a hospital unit based at the famous Scout Camp, Gilwell Park. One small boy who required more medical attention than we could give him was taken to see a doctor. It has to be said that this particular doctor did not have a way with small children. Looking over his spectacles, he asked the nervous child; "How are your stools?" The bewildered boy stammered in reply; "P-Please Sir, I 'aven't got none." Of course, it can happen with people as well as items.

I am reminded again of a time in Shropshire when my wife was working in the doctor's practice. There was a doctor there whose name was also Chris Scott. One day I received a telephone call from one of the other doctors. It started something like this with me answering the telephone; "Hello, this is Chris Scott".

"Hello Chris, this is Patrick".

"Oh hi, Patrick".

"This is Chris Scott?"

"Yes".

And so we moved off into quite a bizarre conversation, me not being at all sure what Patrick (who was a friend) was talking about, and he assuming that he was talking to the other Chris Scott. After a while we realised what had happened, had a laugh and he hung up to 'phone the right number. Same name, different 'object'.

America and Britain have been described as 'two countries separated by the same language'. 'English' is supposedly common to both our countries, yet there are many words which simply do not correspond to the same item. This is also true in many regions of the same country. Local dialect can sometimes make communication very difficult. Not only items, but actions can be given different names, not least when slang expressions are used.

In my last parish, the 'old vicarage', had been empty for a while before it became the new home of an American couple. Before we had got to know one another well, I was speaking with my new neighbours - about gardening and lifting and carrying I think - when I said that Ruth was as strong as me because of all the humping (lifting) of patients she did as a nurse. I had no idea that humping had different connotations in the U.S., and they found their laughter difficult to contain in front of their new priestly neighbour!

In naming some thing, some person or some action we are using a shorthand which makes conversation easier and pigeon-holes things into convenient categories. Yet in doing this we must realise that there is an inevitable lack of precision in what we say. We take it for granted that the other person has a framework of reference similar to, if not the same as our own. When we are speaking about material objects in common use, for most of the time there is little problem in making ourselves understood. When the items become specialised or rare, more care needs to be taken to ensure accuracy of communication. When actions are being described, yet more care is needed, for we are then moving out of the realm of the concrete and touchable into the area of movement, cause and effect. The further one moves from the everyday concrete to the rare and less tangible, the more difficult it is to communicate by using the shorthand of a name.

In the area of the human spirit where cojectivity is experienced as being supremely real, yet beyond our grasp, the use of language and names run into real problems. We have all experienced those arguments about such things as colour.

"She was wearing a wonderful dress, it was an exquisite blue".

"Blue! it was never blue, it was definitely green". And so on.

The area where colours merge one into another is a matter of subjective experience and perception, and different people choose to call the same reality by different names. Yet the reality is the same. No matter what people choose to call a colour, it is what it is by the nature of its reflective properties. With the cojective there is no external reality which is visible, touchable, smellable, tastable or audible. In other words it is not amenable to our five senses, yet it is as real, and sometimes seemingly more so, than the concrete and tangible. As I have said above, it is that which gives meaning to life, a reality beyond mere material existence.

It is not surprising, then, that humanity has given names to the cojective experience, numerous names, but that somehow naming the experience only seems to make communication more difficult rather than less. Of course within particular groups of people the name they have chosen to use binds them in their own understanding (I use the word bind advisedly). Yet it has been my experience that, once you 'scratch the surface' of any group understanding of the cojective, underneath you will find some very differing interpretations. And of course, the more clearly a group defines its experience in the limited form of linguistics, the more it will be alienated from another group who also wish to define the experience clearly, but using different names and words.

In a town which I know quite well there are two churches within a long stone's throw from each other. Both are Church of England, yet it would be true to say that they express their understanding of religion in very different ways, and using very different words. One is High Church Catholic, the other is Evangelical. If pushed, at an intellectual level they will agree that the god they worship (the small 'g' is intentional as will be seen later) is the same one, but that is as far as it goes. It is clear to both groups of people that 'the others' are using words and symbols that are really not a true representation of the god at all. This division between believers of the same faith can be multiplied millions of times over between different faiths, beliefs and viewpoints. And let us not run away with the idea that it is just religious people who so narrowly define the cojective experience. Those who take very different stances can be equally dogmatic and rigorous in their definitions.

In the 1940s and 1950s some of those who followed the

Behaviourist school of psychology insisted that cojectivity and cognition (inner experience and thought) were either non-existent or simply the result of conditioning and reinforcement. By naming their cojective experience people tend to limit and confine it. In this way cojectivity is projected outside as an objective reality to be believed in by other people. Philosophy, religion, science or art can all 'conspire' to make their own particular reality into a universal reality, and the name this reality is given becomes the focus for creeds, doctrines, dogmas and institutions.

In giving a name to anything, even something as everyday and simple as a teacup, what we are doing is projecting outwards from our own complex understanding, which has taken a lifetime to build up, a single word or perhaps a phrase, which we expect the listener to receive in its entirety of meaning. I am sure that you will all have had the experience of being told about something or someone. From the words the other person uses you build up a picture in your mind. What you are doing is creating a reality out of words. Of course, in the absence of the actual person or object, the reality you are creating is your reality not theirs. When you eventually come to meet the person in the flesh, or see the object for itself, your reaction is "it is nothing like I thought it was going to be like". If it is a person you encounter, you may be too polite to say so.

This common experience of being 'misled' by others' descriptions is true of the tangible, solid matter of our everyday existence. How much more so must it be when we are trying to communicate in the realm of the cojective. In all matters of the 'heart' or 'spirit', in all areas where empirical objective proof is not possible, names and descriptions must always be regarded as provisional and never totally adequate.

Each of us has our own unique history, our own perceptions constructed over many years, and our own psychological type. It is only to be expected that our cojective experiences will be described in differing ways, and be given different names. Trouble occurs when any individual or group insists that their particular description or name is the right one. When I was a small boy I thought all foreigners were stupid. At least we (the English) used the right words to talk, they all used gobbledegook! Fortunately I am not quite so jingoistic these days. I have never mastered a second language, but I am increasingly aware of the problems involved in simply trying to use the one that I do have, to build bridges that will unite, rather than create walls of division and isolation.

On a poster that I bought a few years ago, there was a picture of some rather puzzled looking apes. The caption read:

I know you believe you understand what you think I said, But I'm not sure you realise, what you heard is not what I meant.

When we do not understand what another is saying to us, or when we fail to make ourselves understood, we place one more brick in the wall that divides us one from another. Words are so important to the human race. With the utterance of a few words, millions of pounds may be lost or gained, wars may be started or stopped, relationships ended or begun. Both the written and spoken word have enormous potential for good and evil. Yet we tend to be so careless with them. So often there is little thought given to whether or not what we are saying is understood by the listener. And equally, how often do we stop to check out whether we have heard the other person properly?

When speaking with a colleague recently who was very anti-religion, we discovered that in fact, we had very similar beliefs - that is, we could agree on what was fundamentally important in life. Language and words had been a barrier between us before, because we had failed to delve beyond the surface meaning, (a meaning different for both of us). We had created walls by simply not having taken the time to really understand what the other was saying. The bridge we have subsequently built, a bridge that has been beneficial to both of us, is made of the same words, but we gave ourselves time to really listen to each other.

The cojective approach to life is to assume that what we have in common - our humanity - is greater than that which divides us. Whatever other occupation a cojective person may pursue, bridge building will always be a prime objective, and the materials we have most commonly at our disposal are words.

CHAPTER 4
Who Are You?

The title for this chapter comes from Lewis Carroll's Alice's Adventures in Wonderland.

"Who are you?" said the Caterpillar. This was not an encouraging opening for a conversation. Alice replied, rather shyly,

"I - I hardly know sir, just at the present - at least I know who I was when I got up this morning, but I think I must have been changed several times since then."

"What do you mean by that?" said the Caterpillar sternly. "Explain yourself!"

"I can't explain myself, I'm afraid sir", said Alice, "because I'm not myself, you see."

At parties and gatherings, when one is introduced to somebody unknown, the question usually is "what do you do?" rather than "who are you?". It is much easier to define ourselves, and others, in terms of what our occupation is, than to say who we are as people. Again it is a way of classifying and putting them into pigeon-holes, a sort of short-hand for people. I have often wondered what it is like to be a sex-therapist at a party, probably a real conversation stopper. (Although I guess it would depend on the party!)

Yet what we do surely comes second to who we are. Our personal histories, genes, physique and psychology all combine to make some occupations more likely than others. For instance, I think I am psychologically not inclined to want to become Mr. Universe, but that is probably just as well. My five foot eight inch stature, complete with a slight stoop and a not too thin waistline also make it less of a likelihood. It is true of course that both circumstances and perception can prevent a person doing that which is most conducive to who they really are. Many people feel trapped

29

in an occupation or life style that feels repressive, and denies them the opportunity to express their true selves. Repressive occupations need not necessarily be the ones where work is repetitive or uninteresting, but rather ones where the individual finds that they are not able to be themselves. A high-flying lawyer, doctor, or businessman or woman, on an income that most people would envy, can feel less than fulfilled and repressed because they are not being true to themselves. The course of our lives is very often dictated by our social position, our parents' ambitions for us and the education that has been available to us. Once set on a course, especially in a career where long and expensive training is required, it becomes very difficult to change direction. Or if we are in a job that requires little or no skill, and our education and training have not been all that they could be, it is difficult to imagine how things might be different.

In Western society, where our very identity is invested in what we do, let alone our social status, it is often difficult for people to know who they really are. Like Alice they are confused. Part of the 'spirit of our age' is a feeling by so many of 'disconnectedness'. It has been described as a "spiritual vacuum", and many have called for a "return to religion" or for the assertion of "moral values". Yet I believe these calls to be misguided. Both religious beliefs and moral values are concrete and objective expressions of a cojective understanding. They will resonate with some people, but will miss the point with a great many more. Those who make such a call for a return to religion, or the establishment of a particular set of moral values, are simply wanting to make universal a set of beliefs or values which happens to suit them. All too often, these systems or values do nothing to enable the individual to live life more fully and more humanly, and to be able to know the answer to the question "Who are you?" Far from it, such systems and values act as yet another set of external and 'objective' criterion to which the unfortunate individual has to conform.

Now don't get me wrong; I am not anti-religion, nor am I against moral values as such. I am against both when, instead of providing guidelines and possibilities, signposts and indicators, they, or more accurately the way they are used by people, become inflexible systems which pretend to contain the 'truth' for every individual. When this happens, religion and morality become instruments of oppression and conformity, equal to anything that the pressures of an industrialised society or secular state can offer.

The real spiritual malaise which so many people are experiencing, this feeling of disconnectedness and of nothing having any real meaning, comes not from the decline in religion and morals, but from people being alienated from themselves. "I can't explain myself" said Alice, "because I'm not myself you see."

Being separated from who we really are is a death dealing experience. It saps our energy, and, in many people, will lead to sickness and ill health, both mental or psychological and physical. For several decades now, material affluence and security have been pursued as an answer, to fill the emptiness and to give meaning. Like most other things in life, material prosperity is, in itself, neither good nor bad, we can make of it what we will. But to pursue it as the answer to our personal spiritual vacuum is likely to lead to more rather than less discomfort in the end.

Several years ago I remember a colleague of mine relating a conversation he had had with one of Britain's leading industrialists. He said to my friend, "Well, I've reached the top, I've got everything money can offer, but what the hell is it all about?"

To pursue a goal and then to find there is nothing at the end of it is a devastating experience, especially if it has taken you most of your life to get there. The quest for the spirit is a quest for meaning, for fulfilment, both for yourself, and for those around you. To be a truly spiritual person is not to be religious, or pious or even 'nice' (horrible word!), it is to be truly oneself, to be integrated, whole and at-one.

The spiritual quest or journey is not something that is foreign to humankind. It is not some religious peculiarity which entails the suspension of our rationality and the taking on board wholesale of some credal system. Rather, the spiritual journey is that which enables each woman and man, boy and girl, to discover and to be that which they most fully and naturally are. It is as natural to our human state as eating, breathing and sex, but because the word (name) spirituality has become almost exclusively used in connection with, and in relation to, religion and religious activity, it is thought by many to have nothing to do with them. If you are one of those who connect anything containing the word spirit or spiritual with particular religious ideas, this next sentence is especially for you.

THE WORLD OF THE SPIRIT, SPIRITUALITY, AND THE SPIRITUAL JOURNEY ARE DEFINED HERE AS HUMAN ACTIVITIES, THEY ARE THE ESSENCE OF OUR COMMON HUMAN EXPERIENCE, AND THE MEANS OF SELF-FULFILMENT.

Religion may be one way of expressing this fundamentally human activity, and it is a totally valid way, but it is certainly not the only way. And, like anything else, it can equally act as a distraction from the journey, as much as an aid to it. But more of that later.

The seeking to know oneself is often considered in our society as a rather unhealthy thing to do. Those who go to counselling or therapy simply to gain further insight into themselves are sometimes thought of as self-indulgent, selfish or just a little odd. Yet what could be more important than really to know ourselves? If we do not, we will live lives that are likely to be unfulfilled, our relationships with others can never be truly genuine, our motivation for doing almost anything will probably be very suspect, and those with whom we have to live and work will certainly feel the pain of our own fragmented being. Without self-knowledge we are inevitably limited and to some degree at least, dysfunctional people. What we do not know about we have no opportunity to develop, change or control. Yet it is possible that the acquisition of self knowledge can become just another toy to possess or game to play with. Like all forms of learning, the way it is used, positively, negatively, or not at all, is up to each individual. The simple acquisition of self-knowledge is no guarantee that a person will use it to the good, either of themselves or for others.

But without self knowledge we are forever at the mercy of our own neurotic needs, the opinions of others, the current latest fashion, the need to 'succeed' (measured by standards other than our own), our physical good looks and youthful appearance... and so on.

Our lack of self knowledge leads us into a never ending search for meaning and worth which is imbibed from our surrounding culture. Our value is found, not in who we are, for that is an unknown land, but in conforming to an objective standard set by others. And where does that standard come from? It comes from other people projecting outside of themselves their own quest for identity and meaning. This circular activity of chasing illusions can be seen in the hollow looks and false smiles at any social gathering around the world. With some people it becomes so blatant that it almost becomes an art form. State of the art shallowness. I am of course talking about those people fortunate enough to have a sufficiency (and usually a bit more) of the physical needs of life. For those who struggle on a day to day basis for mere survival, the hollow looks come from despair and hunger, smiles when they come are genuine, and meaning is found in a crust of bread or a bowl of rice. The poor know the meaning of life. It is those in countries of affluence who, in the race to be somebody in a material world, have lost sight of themselves. This is no new insight; Hindu religion and Buddhist philosophy call it Maya (illusion), whilst Jesus said "what does it profit a man if he gains the whole world and loses or forfeits himself?" (Luke 9:25).

Notice Jesus says "loses himself". Knowledge of our self is

essential for psychological wholeness; it is enshrined in all the great religions and philosophies of the world, but it does not belong to them. This fundamental truth, that human beings need to know themselves, and then BE themselves, in order to live a substantially fulfilled life in relationship with others, can, is and will be said in many different ways. You may not be into religion, and psycho-talk may give you the heeby-jeebies, or philosophy may leave you cold - no matter. It's there in all the best legends, myths, stories, novels and movies. Knowing ourselves is about embracing both the good and the dark side of our natures; wholeness comes not from escaping from our 'dragons and monsters', but from facing them. (Look what happened to the Sleeping Beauty when the bad fairy was not invited to the party. More about this in the next chapter).

The spiritual quest (the quest for the Holy Grail), is the quest to find ourselves, to be ourselves, and to live our lives as fully functioning human beings. Whatever there may or may not be beyond this life, and objectively we cannot tell that, right now we are human. There can be no higher calling than to live our lives in a fully human way. If we wish to dress it up in religious language, fine, but the spiritual journey is for all of humanity, secular and religious alike. The reality is the same, we simply use different names.

CHAPTER 5
Becoming who I am

In his marvellous little book *Why am I afraid to tell you who I am?*, John Powell answers the question in a nutshell. It is taken from a conversation with a friend.

"I am afraid to tell you who I am, because, if I tell you who I am, you may not like who I am, and it's all that I have."

Fear of rejection makes us put up barriers, for probably the most painful experience known to humanity is the isolation felt when one has been abandoned or rejected. We learn at a very early age that it is better to conform to someone else's standards and patterns, to be accepted on their terms, than to meet with disapproval for 'being ourselves'. From the word 'go', our lives are moulded by our parents and other care-givers who simply apply to us the same standards and expectations applied to them. It is largely an unthoughtout process which repeats the patterns that are familiar, and therefore 'safe'. 'Safe' in this context does not mean that life within the family is good and wholesome; often nothing could be further from the truth. 'Safe' means not having to change anything, not having to think, not having to ask awkward questions about our own upbringing, our standards, assumptions and prejudices. 'Safety' is maintaining the status quo no matter what it costs. And the cost is very high. The cost can be our true self. In this way the saying from the Hebrew Scriptures makes perfect psychological sense. Whilst in its original context it was God who punished the guilty by "visiting the iniquity of the parents upon the children and the children's children, to the third and fourth generations" (Exodus 34:7), we now realise that it takes no vengeful deity to do this. Human beings maintain patterns of behaviour from one generation to the next, probably well beyond the third and fourth generation.

To alter the pattern or break the mould, to question the values and norms of our family and society is a tremendously dangerous business. We run the risk of becoming outcast, of not belonging, of being alone in a hostile world. And so we conform. We continue with the habits and patterns, thoughts and behaviours that confirm us in our role. But so often that role is not really us at all. We spend our lives going against the grain of who we really are, in order not to feel bad about being rejected by a system into which we do not really fit. It is a double bind, follow the herd and be less than oneself, or follow one's own path and risk rejection and loneliness. Because of our conditioning from the beginning, the second choice seldom becomes an option, we just stay with the herd, repeating with our children all the mistakes that were inflicted upon us. Fear keeps us safe, and safety prevents us from becoming who we really are. I am not casting blame here. It is no use blaming our parents, school teachers or any other care-giver for the way we are now, it is simply one of those laws (or lores) of life, that what comes around, goes around.

Nor do I want to imply that everything learned on our parent's knees was intrinsically bad. Living in a complex society requires both knowledge and rules for our survival. "Don't cross the road without looking both ways" is a rule worth holding on to if we wish to live long enough to ask questions about rules in the first place! Nor necessarily are those things which we wish to reject bad in themselves, they may simply not be right for us, or not relevant to our present situation. A simple and harmless illustration of this can be taken from my own home background.

On Sundays at dinner time (which was 1.00pm. sharp), we always had a roast joint of some description, followed almost invariably by a pie - apple, rhubarb, plum, gooseberry etc., with custard - it did not occur to any of us that Sunday dinners could be different. It took the introduction of my brother-in-law into the family to question this ritualistic menu. I think it was probably some hot summer's day, when a light snack or salad would have been more appropriate than a large roast dinner at that time of the day, when he queried the reason for it. I can remember my mother's answer quite distinctly all these years later, "'Cos that's what my mum always cooked at home." Whilst we all enjoyed my mother's cooking, and in itself there was nothing at all wrong with the traditional fare, on occasions when more appropriate food might have been served, it was not even considered as a possibility because we had all become enslaved by Granny's Sunday routine.

Of course in Granny's day, having a Roast on Sunday had some very practical implications. It meant that there was always cold meat in the house for Monday, which was wash day. With no labour saving devices, and a large family (eight children), wash day was an all day activity. From the lighting of the fire under the copper first thing in the morning, to hanging out the last load late in the afternoon, there was little time to stop and prepare food. Sunday's cold meat came into its own. So what for one generation was a very practical solution to a particular problem, became for the next generation a family 'rule' which was never questioned by its members.

This harmless example (none of us was scarred for life by eating roasts and fruit pies), shows how easily we become entrapped by patterns of behaviour from the past, repeating them in the present, regardless of whether or not they are conducive to our current lives or prevailing conditions.

Of course there are those who, for whatever reason, decide to break the mould. Perhaps it was because their parents managed it to a lesser degree and gave them the freedom to be real. Perhaps it was because the pain of being unreal simply became too great, the cost too high, and the risk of exposure became worth it. Maybe it came about as a result of a breakdown, mental, psychological, physical or in a relationship - the end of a marriage or partnership. Or perhaps it was that the partner we chose to live with gave us sufficient love, space and security to begin to let go of the past and become free. There are many reasons why people are enabled to undertake the voyage of discovery towards their true selves, leaving behind them the security of the familiar to venture into the unknown, but whatever their motivation, two things are almost certain.

Firstly there will be, at the least, a lack of understanding from their family and friends, and perhaps outright hostility. All the norms of their life are seen as being challenged by this action, and, as I have said above, keeping the status quo has a lot of energy invested in it.

Secondly, it will involve 'fighting with dragons'. In all of the great tales and myths, the hero has to go on a journey, he (for usually it is a he, but despite the sexist language, it is symbolic of the whole of humanity), encounters many trials, fights and overcomes beasts of every kind, and eventually comes to his destination - to find the treasure or rescue the princess. The fighting with 'beasts and dragons' is symbolic of our own encounter with the darker side of our own personalities. It is something that we would all rather ignore, pretend isn't there, or hope will go away. Yet this encounter is vital to our spiritual journey; without it we can never become truly ourselves, and will always see and hate in others, those aspects of our own personalities we have been unable to face and come to terms with.

In the story of the Sleeping Beauty which I mentioned in the previous chapter, the wicked fairy is not invited to the celebrations of the Princess's birth. What might have happened had she been included on the guest list? Well for sure there would have been an air of uncertainty, people would have felt uncomfortable, and recognition would have had to be given to the power of darkness within the midst. To avoid such feelings of discomfort, she is omitted from the guest list. Yet despite the discomfort that would have occurred, including the wicked fairy would probably have avoided the dreadful consequences which followed. Failing to recognise and include our own 'dark side' has the same destructive results.

The greatest example of this in our present century is the persecution of the Jewish people (and then other minority groups) by the Nazi regime. In the late 1930's the German economy was facing disaster. Instead of taking collective responsibility for the problems, the Nazi element in society projected their own inadequacies and frustrations away from themselves and onto another group, the Jews.

In miniature this is what we all do at an individual level. To a greater or lesser degree, when we fail to recognise our own part in the 'wrongs' of our personal lives, and in the life of society, we project it outside of ourselves on to others. Perhaps it will be known individuals or groups, or more than likely the proverbial 'they'.

'They' should have done something. 'They' always get it wrong. 'They' really means anybody but me.

Part of the spiritual quest is to discover those parts of ourselves we would rather deny. To take responsibility for our own actions, and to realise that whatever the past has held for us, the present moment is our responsibility. We can make of it what we will, but if we choose negative actions with equally negative consequences, we must not try to lay the blame at anybody else's door.

Apart from the psychotic (those who, mentally or psychologically, are not in touch with reality), who are very few in number, there is an almost universal sense of that which is right and that which is wrong. Customs may vary from culture to culture, but these do not usually affect the basic norms of society. The basic behaviours which enable people to live together are enshrined in all the great religions, both past and present. To commit no murder, not to steal another person's property, to honour a marriage relationship (however that is defined), to respect the rights of another, to act with mercy and justice...

Each culture and time in history may express it differently, but at a cojective level, people know what is right. The spiritual journey is concerned with recognising those areas of ourselves that are not fully in accord with all that is good, and taking responsibility for them. It is equally concerned with finding ways in which individuals can be truest to themselves, whilst at the same time seeking the highest good for others in society. The spiritual journey cannot be taken alone. The very nature of the human spirit is that it is experienced most fully cojectively, and not in isolation. People who are intent on themselves, either on their own personal salvation and piety, or on their wealth and power and personal status, are far from the reality of the spiritual life.

The spiritual journey then is to discover as fully as possible who I am as an individual, to be true to that self, regardless of the conditioning of the past or the pressures of the present, and to live my life as fully as I can. But always, always this is done in the interaction with others - at home, in the office, at school, in the factory, on the farm or in the monastery - and with the best interests of others at heart. Spirituality is a here-and-now thing, a fully human thing. It is what brings out the best in people and makes for creative and happy lives. But it doesn't just happen.

Like any art, and learning to live our lives fully is an art - like any art - it requires practice and discipline. Nobody becomes a proficient artist or a concert pianist just by wishing it would happen, a good deal of time and effort has to go into it, and usually more than a little heartache. If you wish to live your life fully, then it will require just as much dedication as if you wish to master an art, sport or any other discipline. The difference is that the spiritual journey is a life-long one. So great is our potential that we will never fully reach it in the average 70 or 80 years that we live.

Most of us have encountered people who have spent their lives on a spiritual journey (whether or not it has any religious content). They tend to be open, flexible, full of love and compassion, interesting and a great joy to be with. We have also encountered those who have taken the opposite path (again, whether or not it

40

has any religious content). They tend to be narrow, bigoted, self-centred, mean, boring and a real pain to spend time with.

Within us all we have the potential to become either fully human and fully alive, a joy to ourselves and those around us. Or we can become mean, self-centred and only half alive to the joy of living. The choice and the responsibility is ours. The spiritual journey is the way that leads to fullness of living. It is a shared journey, and most importantly, it is a HUMAN journey on which all can venture. It is a journey that it is never too late to start, but beware, leave it too long and your perception will tell you that it's just too difficult, not worth the effort, or that it does not exist at all. The longer that you have spent defending the status quo, in making and finding your personal value outside yourself, then the harder it will be to change direction. As Gerald W. Johnson so aptly puts it, "The closed mind, if closed long enough, can be opened by nothing short of dynamite."

Those readers who remember *The Last Battle* by C.S.Lewis will recall that toward the end, a group of Dwarfs are convinced that they are captive in a dark and smelly stable. In fact they are free in the fresh air and daylight.

'Are you blind?' said Trinian.

'Ain't we all blind in the dark?' said Diggle.

'But it isn't dark, you stupid Dwarfs,' said Lucy. 'Can't you see? Look up! Look round! Can't you see the sky and the trees and the flowers? Can't you see me?'

'How in the name of Humbug can I see what ain't there...

No matter what evidence was placed before them, the Dwarfs could only see what they believed to be the case. Like the Dwarfs, many people have invested too much in their narrow visions, and the defence of the status quo, even to begin to conceive of a different reality.

Many modern films and stories reflect the ancient myths and legends. And no wonder, for they are our story, our hopes and our fears. At the end of Stephen Spielburg's film 'Hook', the grown-up Peter Pan, having been totally challenged and changed by his journey back into Never Never Land, discovers something more of his true self. The film ends with him saying "To live, to live will be an awfully big adventure." Such is the spiritual journey, the journey of 'becoming who I am' - but it's for real!

CHAPTER 6

Never on a Friday

Recently, on the afternoon of Good Friday, two of my wife's cousins came to visit us. We talked for a couple of hours over tea and hot cross buns. When it was time for them to go, the question of having supper arose. They said that they had been out to buy some fish because it was Good Friday. When we said that we were having pork chops, there was a look of disbelief on their faces. Neither of them would describe themselves as particularly religious, yet it somehow seemed 'fitting' not to be eating meat on Good Friday. Whilst Ruth and I, both ordained members of the Church were having meat, our non-religious cousins were keeping a ritual from somewhere in the past. This little encounter took me back about twenty five years to my local pub. Part of a conversation overheard struck me quite forcefully at the time, and has stayed with me clearly ever since. It was one of those conversations which crop up from time to time about going to church and being religious. The part that struck home was uttered by a middle-aged lady with a cockney accent. I can hear her now: "Naw, I'm very religious, you'll never catch me with meat in the 'ouse on a Friday".

Despite my youth and lack of understanding, there was a feeling in my bones that this statement was an important one. It managed to sum up all the misconceptions about religion in one short sentence. It is what happens when something cojective gets turned into something objective. Religion is a past master at doing this. It so often manages to turn the great adventure of living, into a set of rules which deny an individual the freedom of self discovery. Rather than becoming a vehicle for a person to become fully themselves, to live their lives creatively as a fully functioning human being, religion becomes a strait-jacket to limit and control. What should set people free to become who they really are, more often than not, to use the (somewhat sexist) words of W.H. Auden, turns them into "tight assed old maids of both sexes". How has this happened? How have the liberating teachings of some great human beings been turned into narrow dogmas which constrict and divide humanity?

One of the reasons that I felt compelled to write this book was the response that I received after writing a short piece for a parish magazine. The article was entitled "Religion is bad for you". It obviously struck a chord with a lot of people. I received telephone calls from those who had given up the struggle with organized religion, but who could identify with living a spiritual life. And many people who, whilst still practising their religion, felt ill at ease with it, welcomed the article as a "breath of fresh air".

Whenever I speak of spirituality rather than religion, I find people who sigh with relief to find somebody who is actually expressing what they feel in their innermost being. It also has to be said that there were those who did not like the article, and found it sufficient reason to cancel their place on the parish retreat which I was conducting that year. But I am not primarily writing for those who are content with their religion, but for those who struggle with it, or simply reject it.

The following passage is the bulk of that article with appeared in the magazine:

Religion is certainly bad for you. At best it helps to contain neurosis. At worst it causes the neurosis and narrow-mindedness which lead to behaviour patterns that are unhealthy and damaging, both to the individual concerned, and to those with whom they come into contact.

I believe this to be true, yet I remain a Priest; why? I remain a priest because I am convinced that the fundamental principle which underlies all the great

44

religions is true. Yet the principle itself cannot be 'captured' within the religion. There is a supreme paradox here, for as soon as the subject of religion is transmitted in anything other than its original form - that is experience - it ceases to be what it actually is. Subject becomes object. Religion has the effect of transforming the reality of experience into a codified system which represents experience, but which is always at least one step removed from it. Religion is healthy only when it is understood as a second-hand representation of an existential reality. Let me give you an example.

You go on holiday to one of the Greek Islands. In your room there is a wonderful photograph of the sunset across the bay - in fact the view from the front of your hotel. Every night you sit in your room looking at the photograph, but never see the real thing. When you return, you tell your friends, "they have the most wonderful sunsets, I can't wait to go and see them again."

Religious belief, like the photograph, is second-hand. It points to a reality beyond itself, a reality which will be experienced differently by every individual. Every religion, and every denomination or sect within every religion has its own 'photograph'. Each proclaims "this is the truth, believe in this". Religion turns subjective experience into objective reality, it bids us abandon real living in exchange for a safe and sterile belief. Believing there is a sunset by enjoying a photo is hardly any substitute for the real thing. I remain a priest because I am committed to the path, not of religion, but of spirituality. Spirituality is not about believing set things, reciting certain creeds, or behaving in predictable ways. Spirituality is concerned with every individual finding their own truth, seeing their own sunset and experiencing their own God. Religion can play a part in this, but only a part, and one needs to sit very lightly to it.

As soon as it becomes important in itself we are drawn into idolatry, into second-hand living. Jesus said to the religious leaders of his day that tax gatherers and prostitutes would enter the Kingdom before them. Why? because in their non-religious way they were seeking the truth, whilst the religious people thought that they had already found it! Religion is bad for you therefore, not in itself - few things are bad in themselves - but when we fail to recognise it for what it is. When we give ourselves to religion as if it is the truth, instead of a (frequently very poor) representation, we remain dead to the truth and dead to ourselves, - for who continues to journey when he thinks he's already arrived? Use religion then as one of your many aids in the spiritual journey, but do not become too attached to it, for if you do, it will surely be the death of your spiritual life.

I naturally speak from the perspective and perceptions of a priest in the Christian tradition. Yet any tradition can become prey to ritual for its own sake, or give it a significance it should not have. Some years ago I occasionally shared in a meditation group led by a Buddhist monk. At the end of the evening he would be given a cup of tea, but it could not be handed to him directly by the lady who was hosting the evening. There was a minor ritual involved to ensure that no contact was made between the monk and the woman. There seemed to me something incongruous about this. Buddhism is very 'hot' on detachment, yet there seemed to be a lot of palaver involved in simply receiving a cup of tea. In ensuring total detachment from women, there seemed to be an unnecessary attachment to ritual. It reminded me of the following traditional story:

> Two Buddhist monks, on their way to a monastery, found an exceeding beautiful woman at the river bank. Like them, she wished to cross the river, but the water was too high. So one of the monks lifted her onto his back and carried her across. His fellow monk was thoroughly scandalized. For two hours he berated him on his negligence in keeping the rule: Had he forgotten he was a monk? How did he dare touch a woman? And worse, carry her across the river? What would people say? Had he not brought their holy religion into disrepute? And so on. The offending monk patiently listened to the never-ending sermon. Finally he interrupted with "Brother, I dropped that woman at the river. Are you still carrying her?"

I am not against ritual; it can add a dimension to life that is very worthwhile. Yet it must never become important in itself. When the ritual becomes more important than people, or when it becomes death-dealing rather than life-giving, then it is time to ask just what we are doing, and why we are doing it. Sometimes religious rituals continue long after they have any reason or significance.

A few years ago Ruth and I attended worship at a very 'high' Anglican church. There came the point in the service when the priest was 'censing' the altar. (For those who are unfamiliar with this practice, 'censing' is waving a container of burning incense [the thurible] at a given object or person). He was wearing a sleeveless garment (chasuble), and as he went round the altar, two other people (the deacon and sub- deacon) were trotting round after him hanging onto his shoulders as though attached with super-

47

glue. Ruth looked totally incredulous. "What on earth are they doing?" she hissed into my ear. This ridiculous spectacle was a left over from the time when the priest wore a very heavy 'sleeved' chasuble. The deacon and sub deacon accompanied the priest, holding up the heavy garment so that his arms were free to swing the thurible. What was once a practical necessity, had turned into an empty and rather ridiculous ritual. It reminded me of another wonderful story, this time from the Hindu tradition.

> When the guru sat down to worship each evening the ashram cat would get in the way and distract the worshippers. So he ordered that the cat be tied up during evening worship. After the guru died the cat continued to be tied up during evening worship. And when the cat died, another cat was brought to the ashram so that it could be duly tied up during evening worship. Centuries later, learned treatises were written by the guru's scholarly disciples on the liturgical significance of tying up a cat while worship is performed.

As I write this chapter I am aware of very many examples where ritual practice has become divorced from original meaning.

To do something 'religiously' has come to mean according to a fixed routine, or with unswerving loyalty to a habit. Far from enabling people to explore their cojective experiences together, religion has discouraged exploration in favour of belief in certain 'objective' criteria. Scripture, creeds, doctrines and dogmas have become an end in themselves, actually preventing and proscribing the possibility of growth and development in those who hold rigidly to them.

Over the years we have seen the horrendous results of religion taken to extremes. In 1978, nine hundred and fourteen people died in a mass suicide action in Jonestown, Guyana. April 1993 saw the horrific tragedy of the Davidian Sect in Waco, Texas; the deaths of men women and children under the influence of the psychopathic 'messiah' David Koresh. And in October 1994 forty eight people died in the sect known as the Order of the Solar Temple. All took literally the apocalyptic books of the bible (books which should be regarded more like fiction than prophesy) which led to a doomsday scenario. And a doomsday scenario was exactly what was planned in Japan by the Aum Shrinri Kyo cult when they released a lethal nerve gas into the Tokyo subway in March 1995.

These are extreme cases of what happens when religious belief and loyalty overrides the need for the individual to discover and explore his or her own path. It is an example of the need for security and certainty, along with a literalistic interpretation of the bible, or other religious text, being exploited to the nth degree. Yet these are but the extreme form of what most religion sets forth in a more diluted form. Whether it is the traditions and creeds of the Catholic Church, the reliance on scripture of the Evangelical Church, the experience of the 'holy spirit' in the charismatic churches, the infallibility of the direct revelation of the Koran in Islam, or being the 'People of God' of the Jewish tradition...

Every religion in some way objectifies the truth in a set of writings and practices, and actively discourages its followers from looking beyond its own boundaries. The result of this is any number of religions and sects, all of which claim to have, if not the monopoly, certainly a clearer vision of the truth than anybody else. In a world that always has been, and always will be, an uncertain and dangerous place, the certainty offered by religion can be a refuge for a person who feels uncertain about him or herself and uncertain about the world in which he or she lives. Yet I believe religious certainty to be a contradiction in terms. As many atheists have pointed out, there is no proof for the existence of God. We 'know' of God experientially not empirically, and two people's experiences can be totally different from one another. The old certainties of religion will no longer do (if they ever did), because they fail to be true to the human spirit, which will not, and cannot, be confined by systems and patterns of belief. The cojective spirit within each person is diminished if it is prevented by a belief system, no matter what form it takes, from 'connecting' with another human being.

As I have pointed out above, people can be 'religious' about more than just religion. Science, politics, materialism or 'good works', can all take on the nature of religion when they become an end in themselves. The 'New Age Movement', which in many ways is a response to, and a rejection of conventional religion, is as prone to the dangers of confining the truth as anything else. The 'alternative society', if it fails to take into account that which it is an alternative to, will be as lop-sided as that which it has rejected. Each swing of the pendulum from one set of values to another, inevitably gets the balance wrong again, but in the opposite direction. The spiritual path is about finding balance, finding and using those things that are valuable to us, and rejecting others. No single religion or belief system has the balance right. We need to discriminate and find those things that resonate with our own spirit, and enable us to live our lives to the full. To paraphrase a certain well known Jewish rabbi; 'Religion is made for humanity, not humanity for religion' (See the Gospel of Mark 2:27).

For those of you who are religious by upbringing or inclination, let me ask you this question. How much of what you do or say in worship do you know the reason for? It is a question worth asking yourself, for it can lead to a greater understanding of what you do, and a liberation from unnecessary clutter. One last story to illustrate religious clutter.

In one church I knew (like many others) the choir always turned to face the altar when they said the creed. All new members of the choir were taught to do the same. On asking, I found that nobody knew why they were doing it. To add to this there was a nave altar in use, so that when they turned, they faced away from the altar being used. And just to make a complete nonsense of the whole thing, the axis of the church was reversed, so that instead of facing East (the traditional reason for turning), they were in fact facing West. As far as I know, they still face West with their backs to the altar on saying the creed. The guru's cat would have been proud of them.

In the second part of this book I shall be looking at ways in which we can practice religion without becoming religious. As I have stated above, religion is certainly one way in which the spirit of humanity can legitimately find its expression. It is not religion that is bad, but an exclusive and dogmatic attitude which can often accompany it.

For those of you who enjoyed the stories of the two monks and the guru's cat, I recommend Anthony de Mello's book *Song of the Bird*. It is an anthology of traditional stories from all over the world.

CHAPTER 7
Saying "Go!" to God

A few years ago, I was asked if I would play the part of Thomas á Becket in T.S. Eliot's *Murder in the Cathedral*. I had never performed in public before, and so was somewhat hesitant at the beginning. But the director/producer Arthur, a man of almost twice my years, had so much enthusiasm and energy that some of it rubbed off on me. And, after all, it was the only time I am ever likely to wear a bishop's mitre! One of the scenes involved me 'wrestling' with the tempters, characters from my own past who tried to seduce me back into the ways of worldly power and grandeur. The second tempter is dismissed with these words:

No! shall I, who keep the keys
Of heaven and hell, supreme alone in England
Who bind and loose, with power from the Pope,
Descend to desire a punier power?
Delegate to deal the doom of damnation,
To condemn kings, not serve among their servants,
Is my open office.
No! Go.

There was tremendous power behind that last line. A dismissal that was final and unmistakable. And it is that sort of dismissal which we need to be able to use for God. To dismiss God with all the force at our disposal. There are three reasons why I believe the spiritual life demands this.

The first point that I want to make is that if there is a God, and that is going to remain an open question throughout this book, there is no way in which we can know, in an empirical or scientific sense, of her existence. There is nothing objective about our knowledge of God; rather, people have experienced something cojectively which they have then called God (or whatever name a given religion may use). Certainly there is much religious practice and liturgy, as well as many scriptures, doctrines, creeds and dogmas, but these objective manifestations are humanity's wish to make concrete that which is deeply important, yet insubstantial. But the fact remains, that there is nothing, no evidence of any sort, that points to the universally accepted position that there is a God. If this were the case, two things would be evident.

One, that there would be far greater unity of belief. The present diverse nature of religious belief points to the fact that there is nothing objective about God. Even given what we know about perspective and perception, there would certainly be more universal agreement about the nature of God, if God was objectively knowable. Two, that if there were any universal and objective evidence for the existence of God, then apart from those who might not be considered quite sane, there would be no possibility of anyone holding the position of an agnostic or atheist. But the fact is, there are millions of people in the world who find either agnosticism or atheism the only credible position to hold.

But in saying "Go!" to God, I am not taking up the position of the atheist, for it seems to me that atheism is as dotty as total and unquestioning belief. We can no more prove that God does not exist, than we can prove that she does. To prove the existence of something may be difficult, to prove its non-existence is surely quite impossible. In saying "Go!", I am arguing for the letting go of our old stereotypes and ideas about God. You may have found it amusing, irritating or affirming that above, I have been referring to God as she. Of course it is silly to call God she, but it is no more silly than referring to God as he. To use gender terms for God just shows how limited is our imagination. It will probably be thought of as nearly blasphemous to speak about God and sex in the same breath, but if we insist on using gender terminology, then we cannot

54

avoid the obvious sexual connotation. To use the term 'he' and 'father' is to indicate that God is a male. So we can ask the question; "Does God have a penis?". If the answer is yes, it is immediately followed by the question "What for?" If the answer is no, then we can ask; "In what way do we mean that God is male?" It becomes clear when we ask simple questions about God's genitals, (or lack of them), that we have made God in our own image. This is not to say that we have "made up" God, as I have said above; we lack evidence either way about God's actual existence. But what we have clearly done is to image God in human likeness.

In early and primitive religions, the person or persons of God was often portrayed in female form. The Goddess was seen as the 'great womb' out of which all life originally came. As man's part in procreation was realised, so the Goddesses acquired a consort whose status gradually grew. In the period covered by the Old and New Testaments, it was thought that the male had all the potential for new life. Like the seed of a flower, the 'seed' of man only needed a fertile place to grow. Woman was reduced to the status of a 'grow bag' and, like a spent grow bag, a woman was referred to as barren if she could not have children. With the process of creation being seen as totally a male thing, it is no wonder that God became a male figure. It is interesting to note that in Hinduism, where both the male and female genitals are symbolically represented as objects for worship, the Gods are both male and female.

Not only does the sex of God come from our own cultural understanding, but so does everything else. God as Lord, King, Majesty, Warrior, Servant and Priest, all come from our human conditioning and experience, which we then project upon the 'person' of God. In the chapter 'What's in a name?' I referred to God with a small 'g'. This is because whatever the reality of God may or may not be, those who differ about it are not differing about the reality (or lack of it), but about their image of God.

From the cojective experience of each group, an image of

55

God has been constructed, which is then worshipped and served as though it were real. Now there is nothing wrong with that, as long as we realise that that is what we are doing. If there is a God, then it, she or he can never be objectively known, only cojectively. To turn our cojective experience into an objective reality is to produce an idol. Hindus, Muslims, Christians and Jews, as well as many other faiths and sects all claim that they have a revelation of the nature of God. Yet all are different. Either one is right and all the rest are wrong, which seems very unlikely, or all have a partial truth, or all are totally wrong. To approach religion cojectively is to realise that each person or faith has an experience which is then culturally and historically expressed in objective form. Whatever the truth of the original experience, its objective expression will always be second-hand, at least one step removed from the experience itself. Cojectivity allows every person to experience their own truth and express it in their own way. It never wants to convert because it realises that one set of second-hand experiences is no better than any other. The cojective person seeks to look beyond the objective manifestation to the experienced reality which lies beyond it. We need to be able to say "Go!", not to the reality, whatever that might be, but to the limited and inadequate expressions produced in every religion, which when objectified and worshipped as the truth, become no more than idols and totems.

To say "Go!" to God is to allow God to be whatever God actually is, without projecting our own images upon the reality. If we allow God to be God, then we also need to allow ourselves to be ourselves. This is the second reason for saying "Go!" to God. In a previous chapter I spoke about the need to both know and be ourselves. So often, certainly within the Christian tradition, I come across people who are inhibited by their religion, rather than set free by it. People who, in their everyday lives, hold down important and responsible jobs, but on Sundays are reduced to nervous wrecks if asked to read a lesson in church. What is this about?

Why do people feel less at ease in church than almost anywhere else? I am talking here of regular church-goers. The unease of people who are not regular worshippers is evident before the service begins. At almost every baptism, wedding or funeral I have conducted, nervous groups of people stand around outside the church until the last minute before going in. Certainly some of it will be the occasion itself, some of it will be the desire for a last cigarette, and some of it will be the sheer alienation that most non-church people feel about the building and its services. But there is, I am sure, something deeper. It is a feeling of unease about God. The image so often presented by the Church is of a God who accepts you if ...

If you conform to certain standards. If you give a proportion of your income. If you worship in this way or that. If, if, if. There is a feeling of having to deny some part of who we really are before we are acceptable. For many people it has uncomfortable undertones of their family, their school, their work... always needing to be something else, something better than I am. There are perhaps some people who feel that they are OK, that they are loved and accepted just as they are, unconditionally. So far I have not met one.

Even with the best intentioned parents, most people receive the message that to be OK, they need to adapt their responses to the wishes of others, to be less, or more than they really are. But some parents, teachers and others who influence us when we are young, are not well intentioned. They can be cruel and bigoted and have little regard for the well being of those in their care. Whether we have been lucky or unlucky in our upbringing, the effect is likely to be the same, only the degree will differ. We feel the need to conform to standards set by another in order to be acceptable, I'll love you if... And God has been tarred with the same brush. It is not surprising of course, given what I said above about us creating God in our own image. So God becomes the ultimate example of whatever it is we feel oppressed by. The ultimate 'person' for whom we have to conform, and deny a part of who we really are.

But if there is a God, then this surely is the one being with whom we can be totally honest. We do not need to put on our 'Sunday best', either literally or metaphorically, because this being must know us totally anyway. What a waste of time and energy trying to pretend we are something we are not. No, if God is, then we can be ourselves with God. We can swear at God and to God, about God and with God. In the introduction to his book *God for Nothing*, Richard MacKenna tells the story of a bereaved woman who, in her anger and frustration shouts out "Fuck God and fuck the Church." Her "Go!" is couched in earthly language which reflects her true feelings at that moment of despair. If anything is prayer, this is. It is a woman crying out in her need and desolation, she is being herself, being real, and that is the most important gift we can offer any other being, human or divine.

Being able to say "Go!" to God is an important part of our spiritual life. It enables us to let go of images that will always be inadequate expressions of a cojective experience, and it allows us to be real and be ourselves, rather than conform to yet another external value which may not be our own.

Both of the above reasons for saying "Go!" to God are personal and individual. They enable us to be free from conditioning, which is both cultural and historical as well as personal. We are liberated to discover for ourselves the reality which underlies literally millions of different images and codes of practice.

But the third reason for saying "Go!" to God is perhaps the most important, and is certainly the most universal. Being able to say "Go!" is a recognition by me, thay my brother atheist or my sister Muslim do not need converting, but understanding. It is a recognition that their cojective experience is being expressed in a different language, with different names and images, but that at the heart of it lies the same reality.

If any 'conversion' needs to take place it is in my heart and in my understanding, so that I can see beyond the limits imposed on me by my race, colour, class (or caste) or by my religious or secular beliefs. Not only does the religious person need to say "Go!" to God to be released from the dead hand of conditioning, but so does the secular atheist. You may think this sounds strange, and that the atheist has already said it once and for all. But we all have our 'gods' or sacred cows, beliefs that we hold on to because they have become comfortable to live with. In discussions with atheists I often find that they have very set views about God and religion which they hold on to with the same tenacity as the staunch believer. They have erected an 'Aunt Sally' which is easily knocked down, and enables them to maintain their position without much thought or effort. The atheist and the fundamentalist believer will often hold not dissimilar views about God and religion, it is just that one totally rejects it and the other believes it wholeheartedly. To say "Go!" to God is about being prepared to let go of our beliefs, religious or secular, in order to try and understand the fundamental sameness of the human spirit.

There will be, I know, those within the Christian tradition, and probably within other traditions also, who will say that what I am proposing is a watering-down of the faith. To admit to the truth which lies within the heart of every human being is to weaken their religion to the point of destruction. But what is real strength? Is it having to cling on to limited beliefs for the sake of security? Or is it being open enough to realise that the truth is bigger than any one individual or group can possibly know in its fullness? How many wars and conflicts, how many arguments and broken relationships have occurred, and still do occur, because people are not willing to say "Go!" to whatever they have set up as a god in their lives? To say "Go!" to whatever limits and confines be it religious or secular, is to open up a way for humanity to be creative rather than destructive. It is to seek the middle ground of cojective understanding which unites rather than divides.

When I was a new Franciscan brother, I was rather holy and pious (at least I thought I was!). I did not use bad language, and thought of swearing as a rather 'unchristian' thing to do. After a few months at the largest friary in Dorset, I was moved to the house in Liverpool, which was run at that time by David, a Canon in the Church, and senior industrial chaplain. In the common room was a box on the wall with doors on it and a spotlight above. I did not immediately look behind the doors, but assumed that there was probably an icon or other holy picture within. It came as quite a surprise to find that in fact, it was a dart-board. Whilst playing a game, David missed the vital number and said "oh shit!" This came as quite a shock to me, a senior priest swearing at such a trivial incident. Afterwards we talked about it. Very gently David said that if everybody in the world stopped swearing tomorrow, the world would not be a much better place. But if everybody loved one another just a fraction more, the world would be transformed. I owe a lot to that holy man (he will probably hate that description), because he enabled me to let go of a lot of sacred cows, and to begin the process of seeing things cojectively, rather than in my black and white two dimensional world of right and wrong, subject and object.

Whatever your beliefs, religious or secular, sit lightly to them, pass beyond them to the reality that unites all humankind. It is a risky business, but it will enable you to become more alive to the Spirit of humanity, and your life will change direction - I guarantee it.

Being able to dismiss God, in whatever language is appropriate for us and for our situation, is the beginning of true spirituality; it connects us with what is most real within ourselves, and transcends the limitation of our own restricted vision. It is the start of something big.

CHAPTER 8
Is there anybody there?

This chapter is written for Betty. Betty is a good friend of mine and has something in common with my pin-up girl. Oh yes, even clergymen can have pin-ups. It has to be admitted though, mine does not fit into the Pirelli calendar category. My pin-up girl is Joan Hickson, that wonderful actress who plays the definitive part of Agatha Christie's Miss Marple. Outwardly, both Joan Hickson and my friend Betty share some similar characteristics. They are both of small physical stature, both women with grey hair, and both are in their eighties. But the one thing about Betty that for me connects her with Joan Hickson, is a quality shared with the redoubtable Miss Marple. They both have a mind as sharp as a bacon slicer!

Betty, like many people of her generation, is a loyal member of the Church. But being a loyal member does not mean that she switches off her keen intellectual abilities as soon as she walks through the church doors. Betty has a searching and questioning mind which is not satisfied with simply accepting handed down formulations from a bygone age. Betty both does believe, and wants to believe in God, but the sort of paternalistic being who 'reigns on high' cuts no ice with her. At the end of the twentieth century many people, like Betty, wish to express their spirituality in a religious and theistic way, but they are not prepared to be intellectually dishonest with themselves to do it. They (and I would include myself amongst their number), want to find a formulation or an understanding which does not depend on a first century or medieval picture of God. And, as I have pointed out earlier in this book, a picture is all that we can have.

If God does exist, then by definition, he, she or it will be beyond our total comprehension and the best that we can do is to create a 'picture' that most fully represents our experience, fractional and marginal though it may be. To my fellow theists (believers in a God of some sort) and especially to other Christians, it might seem very shocking to propose that we do in fact create God according to our own experiences and perceptions. But as I pointed out in the first chapter, this creative process is something we do all the time, even with limited and material objects. I cannot see that it can be anything other than that which is beyond our scientific and rational understanding. I am reminded of a story I heard on the radio told by rabbi Lionel Blue.

A man is standing at the edge of a vast cliff; as he looks over, there is nothing that separates him from the rocks 500 feet below. Suddenly a gust of wind blows him over the edge. As he is falling he grabs hold of a solitary small tree growing out of the cliff face. Below is certain death on the jagged rocks. He looks up to heaven and shouts out; "If there's anybody up there, please help me." A voice from heaven replies; "Just trust in me, let go of the branch and I will catch you in my arms." After a short pause, the man looks up again and says; "Is there anybody else up there?"

All too often people give up their belief in God because God has not come up to their expectation. Prayers go unanswered, innocent people suffer, religion becomes unhelpful or the experience of God simply disappears when it is most needed. But if we realise from the outset that our picture of God is incomplete, that it is constructed from, as it were, no more than the ripples in the water after a boat has passed by (the evidence of something as yet unseen), then, when God fails to live up to our expectations, we can review our picture of God rather than necessarily throwing out the whole concept. In the 11th century, Saint Anselm constructed an argument (the ontological argument) for the proof of the existence of God. It ran something like this:

God (by definition), is that than which nothing greater can be thought. Yet that which actually exists (has being), is greater than that which only exists in the mind by thought. It follows then, that if God is the greatest thing that can be thought, and that actual existence is greater than thought, God must actually exist. Or put more simply; Actual being is greater than just thought. God is the greatest thing we can think of. Therefore God must actually exist because existence is greater than thought.

I admit that this is rather a mind-bender, and not the sort of thing that everyone wants to spend their spare time chewing over. It is though, a very neat proposition, and philosophers have argued about it from that day to this, and logically it works. But logic is not enough. Neither God, nor anything else, can be argued into existence if it does not already exist. Anybody who wants proof for the existence of God is going to come unstuck, at least, if the sort of proof that is required is concrete, tangible and incontrovertible.

Yet there are other areas of life which are just as difficult to prove the existence of, but nevertheless, we take them quite for granted as actually existing. Love and hate, beauty and ugliness are 'facts' of life that we live with on a day to day basis. Yet we are no more able to prove their objective existence than we are able to prove the existence of God.

Love and beauty, hatred and ugliness are experienced as existing, not just by the individual, but cojectively by the whole of humanity. Certainly it is true that any particular expression of these things will not be universally accepted, but the underlying truth that love and beauty, as well as hatred and ugliness do actually exist, will, by most people, be taken for granted. It is the fact that we experience these things, and that the experience is shared with others, that makes them 'realities' for us. It seems to me that, if we are prepared to accept the existence of love, without there being any objective reality outside of ourselves, then there is no reason for dismissing the existence of God by using the same criteria. I have my own 'proof' for the existence of God which, rather than being based on logic, is based on our everyday experience as human beings. It follows these lines:

Love and beauty are, through our experience, known to exist. However, love and beauty cannot be proved to exist, nor can they be proved not to exist. Therefore, that which is known but cannot be proved to exist or not to exist does, through our cojective experience, actually exist. God is known through experience to exist, but cannot be proved to exist or not to exist. Therefore, using the same criteria as for love and beauty, God does actually exist.

This form of argument from experience cannot of course prove the actual and objective existence of God. What it does do though is to prove (to my satisfaction at least) that God is at least as real as love and beauty. As love and beauty and other cojective experiences are those things that give a great deal of meaning to life, we can say that God, through the cojective experience of humanity, actually exists to at least the same degree as the most meaningful realities in the lives of human beings.

So if it is as reasonable to believe in God as it is to believe in love and beauty, what sort of a being is it that we can believe in? Well I guess that if I am being true to what I said earlier in this chapter, I cannot speak in universal terms, but rather I must paint a 'picture' which is personal to me. My hope is though, that because cojectively there is a shared experience of God, my 'picture' will also resonate with you, for perhaps you bought this book in the first place because your 'picture' of God does not fit the religious stereotype. I fully realise that my 'picture' of God will not suit everybody, and to some it will seem like a rejection of traditional teaching. Be that as it may, I offer my 'picture', not because I want to convert anybody or persuade others of the rightness of my view, but simply as an alternative perception. And there must be room for alternative perceptions because, if God exists at all, and if God is infinite (as traditional formulations state), then it must mean that as finite beings it is impossible to have anything other than a partial and incomplete perception. By definition, the infinite cannot be known by the finite.

At the beginning of the previous paragraph I asked the question, "what sort of a being..?" The key to my understanding of God, is that God is not a being at all. To think of God as a being, no matter what descriptive clauses we apply, such as infinite (can a being be infinite?), omnipresent, omniscience etc. is to make God into one being among others.

At our daughter's nativity play a few years ago the children sang some of their favourite songs. In one of them the line ran; "My God is so big, so strong and so mighty, there's nothing that he cannot do." During the singing, the children did the appropriate actions, flexing their muscles to show how strong God is. Of course, along with the rest of the parents, I loved it, my heart melting like butter on a summer's day. But as children grow into teenagers, and teenagers into adults, the idea of a God who is so strong, big and mighty that "there is nothing that he cannot do", does not square with the reality; famine, starvation and mass death. Such a being is either not so strong and mighty after all, or the way in which he chooses to operate leaves a great deal to be desired.

When one looks at the world, both historically and in this present time, it is easy to conclude that if God is a strong mighty being who is somehow 'in charge', then he really hasn't made a very good job of things, and that his morals could do with improving. But what happens when we delete the single word 'a'? We then talk about God not as a being, but simply as Being. This is far more difficult for us to grab hold of; a being has attributes, we can talk about what a being can do, or is like; but just Being? How do you begin to describe that? Well of course you can't, and, from my point of view, that indicates that we are more likely to be on the right track, for as I have indicated above, it is not possible for the finite to know or describe the infinite.

I realise that God as pure Being is not a very comfortable

thought; it takes away the relationship which is possible with 'a being', it makes the idea of prayer much harder (more about that later), and it removes the possibility that 'our' God is the only 'right' God to worship. Yet whilst the concept of God as pure Being is less tangible (not that God is ever really tangible), and reduces our levels of certainty, it also opens up new possibilities which are denied to us when we are limited by the idea of God as a particular being. God as Being is a unifying experience. Regardless of the way in which we choose to worship God (or not), whatever religious path we tread (or not), God as Being becomes the highest common denominator for all of creation.

We all share our being with Being itself. In other words, all things and people who exist (or have being) do so by the very fact of Being. Without Being we would cease to exist. So God as Being necessarily breaks down barriers. There is also a sense of unity for the individual, a sense spoken of by the mystics in all religions, and an insight held in primitive pagan beliefs. We are truly at one with the whole of the cosmos, simply because we 'be' together. God as Being is, at one and the same time, completely other than ourselves, but also supremely personal, the core of my very own being. The difference between understanding God as a being, or as Being, is for me, like the difference between being in love and actually loving.

When we fall in love with another person the experience is dynamic, what I would call a 'white water experience'. We cannot get enough of the other person and our ardour is great, (sexual ardour and religious ardour are not so far apart as you might imagine). But how much are we actually loving the other person? Is it not a projection, an image that we are in love with? At the beginning of a relationship we know very little about the actual person that we have fallen in love with; rather we love what that person represents for us. Only given a great deal of time do we begin to know what the other person is really like. The divorce rate is so high in Britain, and in other western countries, simply

66

because people marry an image which seldom matches the reality of their partner.

Unless couples are prepared for the hard work of getting to know one another, and loving that person instead of the image, then the partnership is doomed from the beginning. But when we do let go of the image, the projection of our own wants and needs, and really love the other person for whom he or she is, instead of who we would like them to be, then the relationship is altogether changed. Gone is the white water experience of not bearing to be apart for a moment, and in its place is the love that is like deep still water, whose depths are unfathomable.

Understanding God as a being is a projection of our own wants and needs; it is in fact to have an image of God who may or may not come up to our expectations. Relating to God as Being is to have let go of our projections, and to have entered into the deep mystery of Being itself. My being in total Being. As in a loving human relationship, which has developed and deepened over time, language is insufficient to express the depth of integration that one feels. But such a depth, which from the outside can look like nothing compared to the activity of 'being in love', is where the human heart connects at its most meaningful level. But to reach this point is not possible if we cling with our whole being to an image which is always created in our own minds, and to fulfil our own needs.

God understood as Being in its fullness is totally personal. God is known, not as we know an object, a chair or a lamp or a bicycle; this is simply to know about something, there is no communication between a person and an object. We know about an object, but it can never know us. Only between persons is there the experience of cojectivity, being known by that which we know. Meaning is given to life not through objects, things, possessions; but by the meeting of heart and mind between two persons.

God as a being becomes another object onto which we project our hopes and fears. We know about this God only because

67

we have created 'him' in the beginning. But God as Being is experienced as both supremely at the centre of my own being, but also as otherness, the source of all being. God can never be known as an object because objects cannot be known, only known about. It is a paradox, a mystery. But life is full of such mysteries.

The paradox is experienced by lovers in the act of making love, not just having sex, but making love. In the physical giving of one person to another, and especially at the point of orgasm, each person is both, at one and the same time, fully self fulfilled, but also fully at one with the other person. So it is with God as Being, we are at one with ourselves, and at one with the source of all Being. For me then, God is real and God is personal because the most real things in life are not objects to be known about, but persons with whom cojective experiences are shared.

In the marvellous interview given for the Face to Face series on BBC television some years ago, Carl Jung the psychiatrist and psychoanalyst was asked the question; "Do you now believe in God?" After some moments of reflection, Jung, who was by no means conventionally religious replied; "No... I do not need to believe; I know."

In the cojective activity of humankind, God as Being is simply present; belief is unnecessary because every single human being experiences Being in and through their own being in the world. Whether or not we choose to give Being the name God, matters not one iota; for Being will be, and we will share in it, regardless of the name that we use to describe it.

Some may object and say that I am not describing God at all, but just the experience of being human. Well yes, of course. I am a human being, my experience is that of being human, I share with other humans, the language I use is human... Yet humans have, from the beginning of recorded history, struggled to express their feelings of knowing and being known, and that behind our being is greater Being.

I can say no more than this; that along with other human beings I experience, cojectively, meaning which extends far beyond the bounds of objective matter. Love, which has no material substance, is more real to me than the car I drive around in (in a few years my car will cease to exist). In the same way, I experience my being as part of greater Being, and like love, it gives meaning to my life. This Being I choose to call God.

We can worship then, Betty and I, in a pretty traditional way. What we are affirming is not that we believe in a being 'out there' somewhere, but rather that life has meaning for us, and that this meaning is shared with others cojectively, so that we have our being in Being itself. We are united in the Spirit of Being where meaning has its ultimate source. Whatever we choose to call God, God will always remain an utter mystery; but what we experience will always be more real than any object ever can be.

"God" said Saint John, "is love"; and love is the cojective experience of humanity which gives meaning to life. Love is a state of being, and Being is what we call God. In the end it is simplicity itself.

As human beings our aim is to live and share a life of love, for love gives meaning and purpose. We need not speculate on the nature of God, nor even bother to argue about God's existence. Love is our contact point; when true love is shared between human beings, then we experience something of the divine, and God is seen on earth.

CHAPTER 9

"Hello Wall"

"Hi ya wall". So starts the film version of Willy Russell's 'Shirley Valentine'. Shirley, the 42 year old Liverpool housewife converses with "wall". It is "wall" that she complains to, "wall" that she confides in, and "wall" that she shares the company of her glass of wine with. When her husband Jo arrives home and finds her talking to the wall, he thinks she is going "round the bend".

One definition of madness is of course being out of touch with reality, and many would argue that talking to a wall is just that (although given Shirley's mind-numbing existence, talking to "wall" would be a very sane thing to do). But what is the difference between talking to "wall" and prayer? The atheistic observer would say that there is no difference, except that in talking to a wall there is at least something there, whereas prayer is a total illusion; there is no reality to match the concept.

Yet for religious people of all persuasions, billions and billions of people worldwide, prayer is, if not a daily occurrence, something that happens very regularly. Even Buddhists, who do not subscribe to a god as such, practice what looks very much like prayer to many believers in God. So what is it that people who pray are actually doing? Is it massive self delusion? Are we all crazy, "loop-the-loop" like Shirley Valentine? Is there room for 'prayer' in the life of the non-believer, those who wish to affirm a spiritual dimension to life without becoming religious about it?

I guess the place to start this particular enquiry is with the traditional notion of prayer; that is, an individual or group 'talking' (although not necessarily out loud) to God who is a being in heaven. It is reckoned that this all powerful being listens to the prayers of 'his' people and answers them. Sometimes it is believed that the prayers are granted, sometimes denied, and sometimes answered in ways that were not expected. By this reckoning, God always answers prayers for the best, because 'he' knows what is good for 'his' children.

The critical observer will note that God cannot lose; whatever happens, good or bad, God is understood to have answered the prayers of the faithful in the way that is best for them. In many ways there seems to be little difference between this and random chance. The non-believer will attribute things to the 'luck of the draw', the believer to the 'will of God'.

As I have stated in the previous chapter, I cannot accept the notion of God as a powerful being somewhere 'out there', who interferes in the lives of human beings in a somewhat random manner. I have heard Christians say to me that an ailment as trifling as a cold has been cured by God because it was prayed for. Personally I am outraged by the idea of a God who would intervene in such a particular way, over such a piffling matter as a head cold. If God has that sort of control and power, what on earth is 'he' doing curing some pious Christian of a head cold, whilst leaving millions of famine victims to starve to death on the other side of the world?

My wife Ruth is an ordained priest in the Church of England. When, in November 1992, the General Synod voted for the ordination of women to the priesthood, nobody was more delighted than I. But I have to say that the fuss that the church has made about it, and continues to make, makes me heartily sick. God has been bombarded with prayers and masses and vigils from people on both sides of the divide. Prayers for the will of God to be done, and for the guidance of the Holy Spirit, have been directed heaven-ward for months and years.

For so many people in the Church of England, and in other churches too, it has taken up huge amounts of time and energy trying to discern the 'will of God'. Apart from the matter of justice for the equal rights and responsibilities of women, which is certainly an issue, in fact the issue, I cannot believe that a God worth 'his' salt would care tuppence (or whatever the heavenly currency might be) about the ordination of women (or men come to that). A God who is concerned with theological niceties and correct doctrines whilst half of 'his' human creation is starving, or tearing itself apart in bloodshed, seems to me to be sick.

A traditional story says that: In October 1917 the Russian Revolution starts. The whole of human history is changed. Millions of people will have their lives altered, many will die, many more will suffer great hardship. In the same month the Russian Church is assembled together in council. Passions run high, great arguments take place, the subject: the colour of the liturgical vestments to be used. Should they be white, or should they be purple?

The concerns of the church, and therefore, the subject of its prayers, is often so parochial that God is perceived as being rather like the boss of a firm, whose interests are concerned more with internal matters and 'keeping the show on the road', than with the wholeness of creation itself. If God is a being, and if 'he' answers prayers in the way that Christians often suppose 'he' does, and if 'his' concerns are about religious liturgy, then, quite frankly, I would rather talk to the wall.

In the previous chapter, I said that thinking about God as Being, rather than as a being, makes prayer more difficult. There is no longer a person, a big Daddy figure with whom to communicate. We cannot expect answers in the same way once God is understood as the one Being in which we all have our own being. In times of conflict God becomes instantly tribal. In the Hebrew Scriptures, there are countless references to the God of Israel over and against the gods of the Hittites, the Amorites, the Canaanites; not to mention (and it isn't) the Araldites (a secular god). In modern times it is no less so.

When the United Kingdom was in conflict with Argentina over the Malvenas (Falkland Islands), prayers were asked for victory by both sides. Both countries are, nominally at least,

Christian; both were asking the same God for victory over the other. God as Being cannot be recruited onto 'sides', can never be partisan, but will be understood just as much as God of the enemy as God of the patriots. God is no longer a 'doer' who intervenes in the world, either for or against us, but is rather the totality of all being and all action, for without Being itself, nothing else would or could be. This makes prayer as an activity extremely difficult. Not only is there not a person to talk to, but what would it be reasonable to say anyway?

As we have seen above, God as an interventionist does not cut any ice, so that petition and intercession (asking for oneself and others) is useless (if we are expecting answers), as is thanksgiving. Certainly being thankful is no bad thing, but can we really give thanks to God for 'his' specific goodness to us?

A person who survives a plane crash may give thanks to God for his survival, but what is he giving thanks for? Surely no one could believe that God had intervened to save him personally, whilst allowing others to perish in the crash. To believe that God especially intervenes to bless or save some people, whilst allowing, or even worse causing, the downfall of others, is beyond my comprehension. This kind of being would certainly not be God, but a god, and if I am going to invest my time and energy into prayer, then I need to feel that I am not wasting my time talking to an imagined deity who has even less substance than Shirley Valentine's "wall".

But if prayer is not an activity; what is it? I want to suggest that it is a way of being; that it has a great deal to do with who we are, but little (except incidentally), to do with what we do. That is not to say that we may not need also to 'do' prayer as a particular activity, either to learn the way of being prayerful in the first place, or as an *aide memoire* to our continual practice. If one thinks of a child learning to write, in the early stages it is very much an activity in itself and goes no further than the learning of shapes. Slowly these shapes take on a symbolic significance and begin to represent words, then sentences and so forth. By the time that the art of writing has been thoroughly learned, writing as an activity in itself is forgotten, has become second nature, and is the means by which communication takes place.

Prayer as an activity is like learning to write. It is something that we do at certain times in order that we might learn the art of simply being prayerful. And as an activity it does not have to mean that we are directing our prayers at another being (God out there), but that we are reminding ourselves of a way of living our lives which is beyond just ourselves. Prayer is traditionally regarded as talking and listening to God. But let me phrase it differently; prayer is allowing my being to become in tune with Being itself. Whether we conceive of Being in theistic terms, or in terms of the wholeness of creation, doesn't greatly matter. The way in which we choose to define Being will affect our practice and beliefs; what it will not do is to affect the reality of Being itself. So what is a prayerful person?

To return to our analogy of writing, one would not describe a writer as someone who practices writing, but rather as someone who communicates through the written word. The physical act of writing (or typing) is by-the-by, it is the means not the end. A prayerful person is, I want to suggest, not someone who spends her or his time in the actual act of prayer, but rather is a person who lives life with a quality of awareness for themselves, for others, and for the environment. In other words, a prayerful person is the woman or man who, in their day to day living, is aware of their part in and responsibility to, Being itself.

Using this definition there are a great many people whom one could call prayerful, yet who are not in the least bit religious. By the same token, there are many pious religious people who are anything but prayerful. If we can get away from the notion that prayer is talking to a being, who will zap us from on high to cure our hang-nails, if only we pray earnestly enough, we can (to return to our earlier analogy), stop practising writing, and start to use it for the job of living our lives to the full.

I am no carpenter; it took me a whole term at school to make a simple tea-pot stand. Yet I do know that it is easier to work with the grain of wood than against it. I am no great swimmer either, but I am aware that swimming with the flow of the water is easier and more productive than trying to swim against the stream. When we become people of prayer (secular or religious), what we are attempting to do is to become aware of, and go with the flow of life; the flow of Being.

Meditation is now practised widely in non-religious settings because it is understood to enable people to function more healthily. People who are aware of themselves, aware of others and aware of the Being of life, are more able to go with the flow, to feel at-one-ment with their fellows and with all of creation. At one level prayer is a selfish thing because it enables us to live more creatively; but creativity, like the ripples in a pond, spreads outwards and will affect all with which it comes into contact. The more creative we can be, the better it will be for all.

I may know little about carpentry, but I know even less about modern physics, yet the theory of chaos resonates within me. If the flapping of a butterfly's wings in England, can, by the ripple effect, eventually cause a tropical storm on the other side of the world, then every action is interlinked with every other to produce either cumulative good or cumulative evil.

Prayer is effective, not because we call upon a deity who intervenes in our affairs, but because it changes our very being into something that more fully represents pure Being itself. Prayer, or at least an attitude of prayer, does actually change things. It is not just talking to the wall, although that may be quite a therapeutic thing to do. (People whose psychological type is extrovert need to 'get it out', to interact with the outside world; if a person is not available to talk to, then talking to "wall" is better than bottling things inside.)

But prayer is not just a release for those of us who are thus psychologically inclined. Prayer is an attitude of being which is actively seeking the goal of union. Like ripples in a pond it works outwards. First we need to be united with ourselves so that we become at peace with who we are. Secondly we need to cultivate an attitude of harmony with our fellow women and men, realising our common humanity. And thirdly, as the ripples extend, we need to become aware of our place within, and our unity with all of creation, so that it becomes impossible for us consciously to abuse the animal world or the environment. Increasingly prayer becomes, not so much an activity in which we are involved, although it may be that as well, but a way of being and relating, first to other beings, and then to Being itself.

But it is not enough to say that prayer is only about being and becoming. I have personally been involved in prayer that has led to physical change and healing. I do not believe that it was God intervening from 'on high', but rather that is was the cumulative effect of people who were attempting to be in tune with the flow of Being itself, and that, when the flow of life is enabled rather than thwarted, things do actually happen. If humankind, no matter what religious persuasion people hold, or whether or not they are religious at all, were to start to live prayerfully, that is to discern and go with the flow of Being itself, then we would see a transformation of this world beyond our wildest imagination.

For those who are wanting to live a spiritual life, regardless of religious belief or not, prayer is an essential element. It is a discipline which we need to embrace if we want to make the journey of becoming who we really are, and becoming one with Being itself. The way that we externally express a discipline of prayer will be different for every individual. What is important, if we are not to create yet more divisions and go against the flow, is to recognise that prayer is not primarily an activity which is easily recognised from the outside, but rather is a way of being which will take many forms.

I know people of prayer who would hate to be thought of as religious; I also know highly religious people who, using my definition of prayer, seem never to have been prayerful in their lives. Being a prayerful person is very much harder than just doing the activity of prayer; it requires that we focus our whole being, all of the time, in the direction of unity with all beings and Being itself.

A saying of Jesus, which is often interpreted in narrowly Christian terms, talks about the way of prayerfulness.

> In everything do to others as you would have them do to you; for this is the law and the prophets.
>
> Enter through the narrow gate; for the gate is wide and the road is easy that leads to destruction, and there are many who take it. For the gate is narrow and the road is hard that leads to life, and there are few who find it.
>
> Beware of false prophets, who come to you in sheep's clothing but inwardly are ravenous wolves. You will know them by their fruits. Are grapes gathered from thorns, or figs from thistles? In the same way every good tree bears good fruit, but a bad tree bears bad fruit. A good tree cannot bear bad fruit, nor can a bad tree bear good fruit. Every tree that does not bear good fruit is cut down and thrown into the fire. Thus you will know them by their fruits.[3]

The discipline of a life of prayerfulness is indeed hard, it runs contrary to the selfishness, greed and narrow-mindedness of our consumer society, where things are loved and people are used. The gate is narrow, not because it is limited to one particular religious tradition, but because it follows the path of love and compassion, something which seems in short supply in our world. Jesus said

3. Matthew 7: 12-20

that "you will know them by their fruits."

People who live prayerful lives, be they religious or not, can be identified 'by their fruits'. Prayerful living is integrated living, and it makes a difference that is tangible. For anyone trying to live a spiritual life, prayer is not an optional extra, it is an attitude of being and becoming which is central to our endeavour. The danger lies in narrowing our perception of prayer so that it becomes a particular form of activity which is exclusive rather than inclusive. Prayer is much more than talking to "wall", it is also much more than religion often portrays it to be. Try it; and go with the flow.

CHAPTER 10
And then there were three

This chapter almost did not get written. Chapters eleven, twelve and thirteen were written before it. I found all sorts or reasons for leaving it out. I told myself that I could get part one of the book to the publishers sooner without it. That nobody would know the difference if it wasn't there. But the more I tried to find reasons for its exclusion, the more it nagged at me. In the introduction I said that if nothing else, this was going be an honest book, and I know that if I avoid writing this chapter, I am being less than honest; at least with myself.

My reluctance to write comes from the sheer difficulty of the subject matter; the Christian doctrine of the Trinity. Over the centuries, reams of parchment and then of paper have been used in trying to explain, expound and elucidate this most difficult concept; God - three in one. We know that there is nothing in the Bible which explicitly speaks of the Trinity; rather the doctrine was created by the early church from implicit references. Some, I have to say, are particularly dubious. The 'sanctus' from Isaiah chapter 6 verse 3 is one such.

And one called to another and said: "Holy, holy, holy is the Lord of hosts; the whole earth is full of his glory."

To start with, taking a 'vision' as some sort of objective description of God seems a particularly dubious thing to do, but even if it could be taken as such, the fact that the seraphs say "holy, holy, holy" is hardly any sort of evidence for God as three-in-one. One might as well say that a policeman saying, "'ello, 'ello, 'ello' what's going on 'ere then" is proof that he has apprehended a trinitarian villain.

But it is not my intention in this chapter to look at the biblical

81

'evidence', nor am I going to go through the way that the church formulated the doctrine of the Trinity. That has been written about to excess already. What I will be doing is to see whether the doctrine of the Trinity makes any sense experientially. What in our lives and experience matches up to an understanding of God as three-in-one?

The idea of God as Trinity comes 'unstuck' when we try to think of God objectively, as though the Trinity actually exists somewhere 'out there'. This is the problem with all doctrines; what is attempted is the expression of a spiritual reality in concrete terms.

A doctrine makes the cojective into the objective, and in so doing, it transforms the original meaning utterly. The phrase 'my love is like a red, red rose' is not an objective statement, but is understood cojectively; the hearer knows what the speaker is talking about because it is, or as been, part of that person's experience too. Taken literally, objectively, it would be a pretty meaningless statement, (unless you were completely obsessed by red roses). So too to talk of the Trinity becomes meaningless if we try to think of it in literal, objective terms. Rather, for those who believe in God, and for those who see Jesus as revealing something of the Divine (more about this in part II of the book), the Trinity is a poetic way of speaking about some ultimate values and experiences. Primarily it is about relationship.

If, as I have suggested in chapter 8, God is not a being, but Being itself, then relationship and integration must, by the very nature of things, be a constituent part. Being without relationship and integration could not exist at all, for nothing would 'hang together'.

Both science and ecology point increasingly to the fact that the world in which we live, indeed the whole cosmos is interrelated; only too slowly we seem to be learning that we simply cannot go on misusing and abusing our environment without it having long term and often unexpected consequences. To be healthy there needs to be balance in the world; this is true not only for an individual, but for families, groups, communities, and nations. Without a proper balance suffering takes place.

For an individual there needs to be a balance in the diet, a balance between work and leisure, between wakefulness and sleep... unless the relationship between all these things is right, then ill health, physical, mental or psychological is likely to follow. And what is true for us as individuals, is also true on a global scale, as well as everything in between. We will never be truly happy, truly whole whilst we in the industrialised nations throw away more food than many nations have available. We shall never be whole whilst there is exploitation of the earth's natural resources for short term gain. A spiritual view of the world is a holistic view, it recognises the total interdependence; it is a view long held, and echoed in those famous words of John Donne:

"No man is an island entire of itself. Any man's death diminishes me because I am involved in mankind; and therefore never send to know for whom the bell tolls; it tolls for thee."

One of the tragedies of modern Western society is the breakdown of community. Much of the suffering which is endured today is directly connected with our increasing isolation. We no longer know who our neighbours are; families live insular lives, not only separated from other family members such as brothers and sisters, aunts, uncles and grandparents often by many miles or even by continents, but the individual family, although living under one roof, is also often fragmented. Not only are the days gone when families would talk together over family meals, play games together and actually communicate, but gone too is the time when the family would gather round the television together.

In Britain today the average home has two television sets, and an increasing amount of time is spent by family members 'doing their own thing', or, more to the point, watching their own programme. I am not against members of a family undertaking individual interests; it is part of the important balance that needs to be maintained, but I do believe that it becomes profoundly unhealthy when people no longer have either the time or the inclination to communicate even within their own family structures. We learn who we are, what value we have, not in isolation, but in relationship with others. I know that I am loved and accepted, which is the most important thing anybody needs to know, not by looking in the mirror, and certainly not from watching the television, but by seeing it in the eyes of another human being. So much of the pain, so much of the violence, so much of the mindless destruction that is part of our modern culture, comes as a direct result of people feeling worthless and unloved. If I feel that I have no value as a person, if I feel unloved and unlovable, then it is impossible for me to love and respect another person. I can give only as much as I have received. Love is a language.

Many a popular song has spoken about the 'language of love', but if I have never learned that language in the first place, I can hardly be expected to speak it. I am dyslexic; as a child at school in the 1950's and early 60's, dyslexia was not known about and not understood. I could not read to the same standard as my peers, could never spell (and still cannot, so thank goodness for the word processor), and simply had, and have, very little facility for remembering certain things.

With the exception of one teacher in my secondary school, a man I shall always be grateful to for the way in which he treated me as a human being worthy of some respect, I was usually ridiculed and/or punished. Needless to say, this did not improve my dyslexia; I spent a great deal of time 'bunking off', and, in my primary school days, the 'school board man' as he was then known, was a constant visitor to my home. Punishment was no answer to my dyslexia; it simply drove me further away from the help and acceptance which I then needed.

Punishment too is no answer to the crime and violence of our present day society; it is treating a symptom, the cause of which

84

is a deep spiritual malaise in our society. I am not saying that symptoms do not need to be treated, but it seems a sick society that only punishes those who have already been victims of that very sickness. No one would dream of punishing a person for not being able to speak a language with which they had never come into contact, yet we expect people to show respect, love, tolerance and understanding when they have never come into contact with that 'language' themselves.

In the rich and affluent societies of the world, there are millions upon millions of deprived children. I am not just talking about those who come from poor homes, from ghettos or slums, although of course there will be many from these circumstances.

Physical deprivation is one symptom amongst a sick society. The deprivation to which I am referring is a spiritual deprivation; it is the deprivation that comes from insufficient and inadequate relationships. There are no class boundaries to this kind of deprivation, no financial limits, no material dividing lines. Some of the most deprived people that I have come across in my counselling work have been individuals from wealthy and upper class backgrounds. The deprivation is not in terms of material 'goodies', but of relationship.

Experiments with monkeys (the ethics of which I shall not enter into on this occasion) carried out by Harlow and Suomi in 1970 showed very conclusively that monkeys raised with artificial mothers had an innate preference for a soft and warm substitute over against one that simply supplied food. But the most illuminating of the experimental results was shown when the monkeys grew to adulthood.

Infant monkeys raised with artificial mothers and
isolated from other monkeys during the first six months
of life showed various types of bizarre behaviour in
adulthood. They rarely engaged in normal interaction

with other monkeys later on.... and their sexual response was inappropriate. When female monkeys that were deprived of early social contact were successfully mated (after considerable effort), they made very poor mothers, tending to neglect or abuse their infants.[4]

The work on attachment by psychologist Ronald Bowlby has shown that what is true for monkeys, is equally true for human beings as well.

The failure to form attachment to one or a few primary persons in the early years can be related to an inability to develop close personal relationships in adulthood.[5]

Close personal relationships are the one crucial factor in the healthy development of people. The abundance of material wealth can be as detrimental to good relationships as is an oppressive lack of material necessity.

There is no substitute for loving and accepting relationships. Relationship means knowing and being known; not knowing *about* someone, or them knowing *about* us, which is simply knowledge of subject to object; knowing *about* is not relationship.

This is the vital spiritual element that our modern society is so bereft of. It shows in our materialism, our rushing after time, our greed to possess. We have lost, or are at least, are in danger of losing, that most precious of human gifts, our spiritual nature, our cojective ability to be at one with one another, and with the environment upon which we depend. We could learn a lot from the contented fisherman.

4. Psychology, 9th edition, Atkinson, Atkinson, Smith & Hilgard (1985)
5. Bowlby (1973)

The rich industrialist from the North was horrified to find a Southern fisherman lying lazily beside his boat, smoking a pipe.

"Why aren't you out fishing?" said the industrialist.

"Because I have caught enough fish for the day", said the fisherman.

"Why don't you catch more?"

"What would I do with it?"

"You could earn more money" was the reply. "With that you could have a motor fixed to your boat and go into deeper waters and catch more fish. Then you could make enough money to buy nylon nets. These would bring you more fish and more money. Soon you would have enough money to own two boats... maybe even a fleet of boats. Then you would be a rich man like me."

"What would I do then?"

"Then you could really enjoy life."

"What do you think I am doing right now?"

In our headlong rush to find happiness in material wealth, a happiness that we are constantly bombarded with by television advertising, posters, hoardings and glossy magazines, we have lost sight of our real treasure - human relationships. Jesus said:

Do not store up for yourselves treasures on earth, where moth and rust consume and where thieves break in and steal; but store up for yourselves treasure in heaven, where neither moth nor rust consumes and where thieves do not break in and steal. For where your treasure is, there your heart will be also.[6]

6. Matthew 6:19

This is a profound spiritual truth; where your treasure is, there your heart will be also. If our treasure is in objects, with which we can have no relationship, then our heart will be there also, bereft of the most vital of all human needs.

We need therefore not be surprised at the violence and greed at large in our society; material gain is where our heart is. Unless and until, in all layers of society, from poorest to richest, a priority is given to loving and caring relationships, especially amongst the young, then we will continue to have all the symptoms of a very sick society, punishing offenders for doing only that which they have been taught; putting their heart where their treasure is - in objects, not in people.

All this may seem very far away from the doctrine of the Trinity; I believe it is central to it. Trinity is about Being in relationship. Whatever the objective truth about God is, and that we can never know, what the Christian understanding brings us is that Ultimate Being, be it human or divine, does not operate in isolation. At the very core of creation is a relationship which overflows with creative love. The Holy Spirit, which has always been regarded as being the feminine aspect of God, is the very spirit of human cojectivity which flows between people as the creative and uniting power of love. The experience of the early Church, their understanding of Jesus and the cojective experience of the Spirit, led to the formulation of the Trinity; Father, Son and Holy Spirit. But we need not regard these words as descriptive of three actual beings, but rather as indicative of the interdependent relationship at the heart of Being itself.

We cannot live a spiritual existence outside of true relationship, both with others, and with our environment. Many psychological illnesses would not exist if people had genuine loving relationships. Conflicts and wars would be far less likely to happen if people really knew one another; for so much conflict is based on ignorance and prejudice. Nor would we rape the very earth upon whose existence we depend if we had a relationship with it. The doctrine of the Trinity then is central to a spiritual understanding, not because it speaks about an objective reality in which we must believe, but because it points to the essential nature of creation; which is one of interdependence in relationship.

CHAPTER 11

Eternity - a divine idea

The idea of eternity, or life after death, seems to be as old as humankind itself. Each civilisation has had its own concepts of a life after this one, often with elaborate preparations, made (by those who were rich and powerful enough) for the journey into the life beyond. Today, there are basically three differing sets of beliefs about what lies beyond death.

First is the belief that nothing at all lies beyond our physical death. The human spirit is understood as being totally bound up with the mechanics and chemistry of our brain and nervous system. When the 'machine' stops, that's it; we simply cease to be. It is a view that demands serious thought because, scientifically speaking, it has the evidence on its side. Although there are those people who have had near death experiences, about which I shall say more later, there is nothing to indicate, beyond anecdotes and beliefs, that life continues in any way once we have stopped functioning as a physical entity. It also has to be said though, that although there is no scientific evidence to support the idea of life after death, there is also a total lack of evidence to say that there is not.

At our present state of scientific knowledge, neither the presence nor the absence of a life after this one can be proved. What we have to go on is experience, belief and conviction, and for some people the balance of the argument comes down on the side of obliteration rather than continued existence.

The second form of belief about our post-mortem existence comes from the Christian, Jewish and Moslem traditions. Within Christianity, although the belief would appear uniform from the outside, there is in fact, a number of differing beliefs around one theme. The central idea is one of a continuing life where, after departing this world, the individual is 'judged'. Depending on how well we may or may not have done, we might either go straight to heaven (without passing Go), or if we have been really wicked, it will be straight to hell for everlasting torment in the fire and brimstone.

Large sections of Christianity believe in a sort of 'half way house' which is called purgatory. In purgatory, those who are not good enough to go straight to heaven get a chance to 'work off their sins' before being able to pass through the pearly gates. Although in these modern times fewer people believe in the heaven of clouds and harps and wings, and even fewer in a hell with brimstone and fire, they are still conceived of as places where people go after death, even if the details are less clear than in bygone times. It is envisaged that in heaven we shall enjoy everlasting life in the presence of God and in the company of all the saints. Hell, if pictured at all these days, is often portrayed as a grey and lonely place, a place of isolation and despair. However they are pictured, this view of the afterlife is one of eternal being in another place.

The third view of life after this one is that of reincarnation, or transmigration of the soul. (Reincarnation is the movement of the soul from one human life to another, transmigration is the movement to or from any life form, human, animal or vegetable to another). This is the view that is predominantly held in the East, particularly by both Hindus and Buddhists. In this view the soul (atman), passes after death into another being; this may happen many hundreds or thousands of times. The goal of reincarnation is that the soul will learn on its many incarnations and, eventually, this will lead to enlightenment. This end point differs for Hindus and Buddhists.

In Hinduism, where there is a belief in God, enlightenment leads to the individual soul, the atman, being reunited with supreme Being, Brahman, from which it came from the first.

In Buddhism, where this is no God, the goal of enlightenment is to escape the continual cycle of birth and re-birth (samsara), and to enter nirvana, which is a sort of beingless bliss. (Nirvana is a state that Buddhists themselves usually decline to try and describe, but beingless bliss points, I think, in the right direction).

From the two basic sets of beliefs in a continuance of life, in heaven (or hell), or reincarnation, come a huge number of variations. Reincarnation does not preclude heaven and hell; in Hinduism they are understood as 'stop-off points' between lives, and Buddhism certainly entertains the idea of other levels of existence beyond this world. Whilst in Christianity, although the 'official line' has always been one of resurrection and heaven, reincarnation is what is actually believed by many practising Christians.

In our pluralist society, where ideas from all the great religions have been circulating freely for the best part of two hundred years, and certainly since the turn of the century, we now have a 'pick 'n' mix' of beliefs amongst people of all faiths and none, so what can we reasonably believe about life after death?

Part of the problem, it seems to me, is that it is reasonable to believe any of the above. The question is, do any of these beliefs actually affect the way we live our lives here and now? Let us look at the first belief, or perhaps I should say non-belief first. If I believe that there is nothing after this life, how might it affect me now?

Well firstly, there is neither fear of punishment nor hope of reward. What you see is what you get. It may be thought that this rather bleak outlook would perhaps spur people on to living a selfish and self-centred existence. An individual might say; "If this is all there is, then let's make the most of it, I'll get all I can while I can, and to hell with anyone who gets in my way".

Well that may be true, but history would seem to point to the fact that when people really did believe in heaven and hell, their behaviour was no better than it is today. In actual fact, some of the worst atrocities inflicted upon man, by man, have been committed by people who thought that they had 'heaven' on their side. No, a lack of belief in the life hereafter does not necessarily lead to anti-social behaviour; in fact the opposite may well be true. If I believe that this is all there is, then there is a great impetus to make the most of life, not only for myself, but for those with whom I share this life. My 'immortality' will rest only in those things that have been creative in my life, things that will stand the test of time and the 'wisdom' of hindsight. To believe that this life is the only one we have does not therefore go against a spiritual view of the world; rather it points to the fact that we need to live life to the full now. It is no good putting things off, tomorrow may really be too late.

A belief that we cease to be at the point of death is not in itself an unspiritual view; what it does do is to concentrate our spiritual living in the here and now, and that can be no bad thing at all. The traditional understanding of life after death 'in heaven' has a carrot and stick feel about it. The reward for being good during our life on earth is everlasting life in heaven. The consequences of bad behaviour or lack of belief is fire and brimstone or some other miserable existence for ever. (My picture of hell is having to move house, you just get everything sorted out, then you have to move again - for ever and ever!)

But however you picture heaven and hell, the idea of punishment and/or reward seems somehow a little less than moral. If I live a good life here, only because I fear hell, or because I hope for heaven, it means that I am not leading a truly spiritual life, being creative and good for its own sake; rather I am doing it only because of ulterior motives. A truly good action does not come out of fear or reward, but is done for its own sake alone. If, therefore, our view of heaven and hell drives our actions, it may well be that we are actually prevented from living our lives in a thoroughly spiritual way; we are, either consciously or unconsciously, more concerned with the long term (eternal) effect on ourselves, than on the action in the here and now.

Reincarnation is a belief held by a very great number of the world's population, and since the beginning of this century, it has become increasing popular amongst those in the West, not least as I stated above, with people who would also describe themselves as members of the Christian Church. Central to the belief in reincarnation is the law of karma.

Karma is simple cause and effect. There is no judge to tally up our sins on the day of our death. Karma works independently of any deity or lack of deity; it is like a set of pan-scales with evil on one side and good on the other. The down-side of this belief is that it can produce an air of fatalism. Suffering in this life is due to evil committed in a past life, an individual has to live through their karma in order to 'balance the scales'.

In the Eastern tradition, spirituality is understood very much in individual terms, with each person needing to balance their own karma and tread their own spiritual path. Enlightenment is reached, and the wheel of re-birth escaped (moksa), not by doing good deeds, but by learning detachment. Goodness in itself therefore cannot bring a person nearer to enlightenment and escape, for one can be equally attached to good things as to bad.

For me, the spiritual journey is a profoundly mutual one, where interdependence with other people and our environment is an essential element. To be too concerned with one's own spiritual journey, at the expense of social action and interaction is to miss out on the greatest source of spiritual experience; which is loving human interaction.

But what of the evidence for a life after this one? From the Christian perspective, people might point to the resurrection of Jesus as a proof of on-going life, but this, it seems to me is hardly valid. Firstly, we cannot be at all sure what did happen on that first Easter day. If one reads the four accounts in the Gospels, the reported facts do not tally. This in itself is not conclusive evidence against the resurrection. Reports written down some time after the event will be expressed by each writer differently, different things will be remembered or forgotten, and differing emphases will be stressed. What we can say, both from the Gospel stories, and from the tradition of the Church, is that Jesus's disciples believed that he had risen from the dead. That this was a physical resurrection, his actual crucified body re-animated, seems highly unlikely, especially given the texts where he is portrayed as appearing in locked rooms.

But whatever the experience was, in itself it does not prove that there is a continued existence after death for everybody. One swallow doesn't make a summer, nor does one account of resurrection indicate a universal truth for all humanity. No, as a proof of life after death the resurrection accounts provide, in themselves, insufficient evidence for us to be able to make any general statements on the subject.

The concept of reincarnation provides us with considerably more in the way of evidence. True, none of it would fall within the category of evidence for either scientific or legal requirements, but anecdotal evidence is quite abundant. Much of this evidence takes the form of remembered lives previously lived, or at least particular facts which are later verified as correct. Whilst it is possible to find alternative explanations to many such accounts, it does seem to me that there are some events which remain unexplainable by normal scientific criteria, and that reincarnation as a possibility cannot be ruled out.

For some people the evidence is overwhelmingly strong, and they have no doubts about the validity of this Eastern belief. For others the evidence carries no weight whatsoever, and any idea of reincarnation is roundly denied. Objectively we can neither prove nor disprove reincarnation as a way of continued existence. It seems to me that to be dogmatic in either direction is to go beyond the available evidence. Like resurrection, it is an idea, a belief, which seems to be a feasible possibility, and one that we can quite reasonably keep an open mind about.

Those who report that they have had near death experiences come from a wide variety of backgrounds and cultures. There are often two aspects of these experiences which point to an existence other than the purely physical.

The first is an 'out of body' experience where the individual reports seeing themselves from a point, usually somewhere above their own bodies, (usually these events occur during acute illness where the patient is, to all external observation, clinically dead or very near death). Some of what they are able to describe after regaining consciousness is hard to account for in any other way than that they were in fact, outside of their own bodies for a period of time.

The second aspect of a near death experience is often described as a journey along a tunnel to a place of brilliant light at the other end. Frequently the 'dead' person will encounter previously deceased friends or relatives, and also a religious figure, perhaps Jesus, or a Hindu God or holy man, depending upon the culture of that particular individual.

In all of the accounts that I have seen, the universal effect of the experience was to make the individual concerned quite sure about a life hereafter, which in turn often had a profound effect upon the remainder of their life. Personally I am more convinced by the accounts of people witnessing their own resuscitation than I am by the accounts of the after life, which may be caused by a severe lack of oxygen to the brain. Again, evidence either way is not conclusive, except for those who have experience of it; they usually have no doubts.

After thousands of years of belief, experience and experiment, it is impossible to prove conclusively that either there is or there is not life after this one. All of the evidence from all of the religions, and I would not want to discount the experiences of spiritualism in this, does not add up to any sort of concrete proof. But add it all together and it seems to me that, although it would be foolish to speculate about the exact, or even the inexact nature of a life after physical death, it is not at all unreasonable to believe that there is a continuance in some form, albeit as incomprehensible to us now, as this life is incomprehensible to the foetus in the womb.

For those who are wanting to live their lives in a spiritual way however, life after this one should be of little concern. All too often, especially within the Christian tradition, eternal life is equated with everlasting life; something that happens after death. But eternity is a very different thing from something being everlasting.

Do you remember everlasting gobstoppers? Those great ball-bearing-like sweets that filled the mouth and rotted the teeth never did, of course, last for ever. But for a small boy with a penny to spend it was heaven. In a very real way the penny gobstopper was more eternal than everlasting. It brought a quality to life which was not about being long lasting (I knew even as a very small boy that it wouldn't really last for ever), but about the moment, being in the moment, living in the moment, making the best of now. Eternity must be understood in terms of a quality of time, rather than a quantity.

This is the nature of eternal life. It is to do with a quality of living in the present moment, it is about who we are now, not what may become of us after we are dead. To live spiritually is to participate in eternity as a quality of being which has a timelessness about it.

In his letter to those living in Corinth, Saint Paul concludes his famous 'poem to love' with these words:

There are three things that last for ever, faith, hope and love; but the greatest of them all is love.[7]

It could be paraphrased as such:

There are three eternal qualities, faith, hope and love; but the greatest of them all is love.

When we speak about something lasting for ever, we speak

7. 1 Corinthians 13

about time in terms of quantity. 'Forever' is beyond our imagination, it is a quantity of time which just keeps on going, a sort of Alice in Wonderland path which rolls out before us, and rolls up behind us as we go. Something lasting for ever is beyond our conception, and certainly beyond our experience. Time as a quality, however, is neither beyond our conception nor our experience. We have all experienced situations where 'time has stood still'. Either we are so entranced and delighted that 'hours pass in moments', or we are involved in some horror where hours seem to go by, but the hands on the clock show only the passing of a few minutes.

Eternity is a quality of life in which we are called, as spiritual beings, to share. The practice of faith, hope and love is the means by which, cojectively, eternity is lived and shared with others. Eternal life is therefore not to be looked forward to as a post mortem experience, but to be lived out in the here and now with our fellow humans, and in the environment of the present day.

Whatever awaits us after our death; oblivion, resurrection or reincarnation does not really seem to me to matter much. If there is life after death, then there is; if there is nothing, then there is nothing. Either way there seems little point worrying about it one way or the other. Too many religious people spend their lives concerned about what will happen after their deaths. What a waste of time! Live life to the full now, in faith and hope and love after death, what will be will surely be, and no amount of religious hypothesising or speculating will make one iota of difference. In the 'Hail Mary', the prayer runs, "prayer for us sinners now and at the hour of our death."

Now, this moment in time, and the fact that we shall die are really the only two things that we can be totally certain about. Between now and the hour of our death, it would seem only sensible, not to count the minutes, but to live a quality of life which is truly eternal.

CHAPTER 12
What in religion is necessary for the spiritual life?

For those of you who are religious by inclination and/or practice, it might come as quite a surprise to hear that I think that nothing whatsoever from your particular religion is actually necessary for the spiritual life.

During this chapter, I shall be arguing from the perspective of the Christian tradition, but I believe that it will be clear that what is true for Christianity, is equally true for other faiths as well. As I have said earlier in this book, religion is a response to a spiritual experience, it comes as a result of a person or persons experiencing the spiritual, and not as a prerequisite to it. Another traditional story gives a flavour of this.

The explorer returned to his people, who were eager to know about the Amazon. But how could he ever put into words the feelings that flooded his heart when he saw exotic flowers and heard the night sound of the forest; when he sensed the danger of wild beasts or paddled his canoe over treacherous rapids? He said "Go and find out for yourselves." To guide them he drew a map of the river. They pounced upon the map. They framed it in their town hall. They made copies of it for themselves. And all who had a copy considered themselves experts on the river, for did they not know its every turn and bend, how broad it was and how deep, where the rapids were and where the falls?

Although a map may be very useful, it is not essential, in fact, it may even prevent us from exploring ourselves. Like the

101

townspeople from the above story, we might fasten onto the map itself, believing that in it, we have all that we need for the spiritual adventure. Or, even if we are not so limited in our vision as that, having a ready-made map may prevent us from doing any exploration of our own. Although we may journey, we will confine ourselves to paths already trodden, and perhaps miss out on discovering that which is right for us, simply because it is off of the well worn path. Our religion is like the map.

There are some people who, having once familiarised themselves with it at a pretty rudimentary level, believe that they have all that they need to know. Religion is practised at arm's length, part of the social fabric of life, but in no way impinges upon daily activity. There are others who study the map more closely, and having done so make a real attempt to follow the route themselves. Over the years of course, the map has been interpreted many different times, and so people who believe that they share the same map, nevertheless find themselves going off in different directions. Despite this rather strange situation, the map is adhered to rigidly, and straying off the path is considered dangerous, and perhaps even sinful.

If one has, for a long period of time, been taught that the map is essential in order to get to the destination, then the idea of letting it go will not come easily. Or, if you have been directionless for a long time, and then somebody gives you a map and tells you that this, and this alone is the answer to your searchings, then being prepared also to look elsewhere will seem like a very risky business. What I am wanting to suggest in this chapter is that no single religion (map) in itself is essential for a person to live the spiritual life. We may as individuals want to hang on to considerable parts of our religious understanding; that is fine. What we need to realise however is that it is essential to us, and not necessarily to anybody else.

Let us look at some of those elements from the Christian

tradition that might be thought to be essential on the spiritual path.

One of the great bones of contention for those who are opposed to the ordination of women to the priesthood is the celebration of the Eucharist, otherwise known as the Mass, Holy Communion or the Lord's Supper. Many argue that because Jesus was himself a man, those who represent him as president of the Eucharist should also be male themselves. This seems to neglect the fact that Jesus was also Middle-Eastern, circumcised, unmarried (as far as we know) and apparently, homeless. Should all priests be the same? But the argument rages because the Eucharist is seen to be so central to the life of a Christian. But is the Eucharist essential for the spiritual journey? The answer is clearly no. If we were to say that participation in the Eucharist was essential to the spiritual life, we would immediately preclude the majority of the world's population.

All those women and men of other faiths and none, who are living out their spirituality in a loving and human way, have no need of, and many have no knowledge of eucharistic participation, yet their spirituality is none the less for that. And not only are there those who are not part of the Christian faith, but there are those thousands of Christians for whom the Eucharist plays no part. Neither members of the Salvation Army nor Quakers participate in the Eucharist as a formal sacrament; but who amongst Christians would dare to say that they are somehow substandard because of it? The Eucharist is a non-essential for the spiritual life.

Well, what about the Bible, surely this must be an essential item? Certainly the Bible is common to Christians of every denomination and theological persuasion, it is the common denominator that runs through a very diverse religion. Yet how common is it? There are many different translations, of varying accuracies. One of the funniest must be an American version of the Living Bible which has Saul going into the cave to 'use the bathroom'. But it is not translation that causes real problems, but interpretation.

There are as many different interpretations of any given text as there are divisions within Christendom. They range from those that are completely 'off the wall', like those in some of the sects which use biblical texts to fit in with the neuroses of their founders (this usually includes giving a lot of money to the so-called church), to the orthodoxy of Rome and the East, where long tradition dictates interpretation.

But even within the orthodox Churches where long tradition and sound scholarship give a more stable approach, different theologians interpret passages in different ways. The Bible is a record of previous people's encounter with God and, like any other tool, it can be used or abused, be either a help or a hindrance in our spiritual journey. Jehovah's Witnesses quote from the Bible to prevent life-saving blood transfusions, and some fundamentalists in America quote from Leviticus in saying that homosexuals should be killed.

The Bible is, and always has been, a mixed blessing. Its misuse has caused as much suffering as its proper use has caused blessing. And not only that, there are holy women and men from other religious traditions and none, who have lived spiritual lives without even seeing the Bible. We might feel reluctant to do it, but leaving our Bible at home will not necessarily impede our spiritual journey; in fact the opposite may well be true.

At the end of "Hello Wall" I said that prayer is not an optional extra, but is central to the endeavour of the spiritual journey. So am I contradicting myself in saying that nothing from our religion is necessary for the spiritual life? Well yes and no. Yes, because prayer as a way of being and becoming is essential; but no, if we imagine that any particular type or style of prayer is required.

Not long after I was first ordained I had a chat with a bishop. He was a caring and loving man, certainly a man of prayer in both senses of the word. As some readers might know, clergy in the

Church of England are required by Canon Law to say morning and evening prayer every day, and not only say it, but say it from either the Book of Common Prayer (1662), or the Alternative Service Book (1980).

Saying the offices (as morning and evening prayer are known) by myself is something that I have never found in the least bit prayerful. I think I would just as soon read the side of a cornflakes packet. We discussed my dilemma and the possible alternative forms of prayer that could be used; he was quite open to my praying in different ways, as long as I said the office first. He said, "If you are quick, you can get through it in ten minutes."

Even then, as a relatively young man and new to the ordained ministry, I felt that this was simply turning prayer into a ritual; it seemed to have much more connection with the strict rules of the Pharisees than it had to do with the teachings of Jesus.

Prayer in any particular form, if it is not enabling your growth as a spiritual person, not only can be let go, but should be let go. Different traditions within the Christian church have their own norms for prayer. There is the "I just want to tell you Lord" approach of spontaneous prayer within the evangelical tradition. Or the 'hands up in the air' of the charismatic tradition, or the silent devotions before the crucifix of the catholic tradition, and many others besides. What becomes destructive to prayer and the spiritual path is when any particular form of prayers is insisted upon as the only proper way to pray. All can be used as expressions of prayer, but none have to be.

Having said that we do not require anything from religion for our spiritual life, I want to qualify it. Nothing is universally necessary. That is, that there is nothing from my religious tradition, nothing that I myself find essential, that will necessarily be essential for any other person. This is an extremely important fact to grasp for two reasons. First, once we realise that that which we find personally necessary to our spiritual life is just that, personal, it will prevent us

105

from being narrow and dogmatic about the way other people find their spiritual path. It is the idea that somehow our way is the best way, or even the only way, that leads to intolerance and bigotry. Once we can grasp the idea that our particular way of expression is not in itself necessary, but only helpful or desirable, then we are able to give other people the freedom to choose their own preferences, without feeling that it in any way threatens the choices that we have made. In this way we are able to learn from one another because, if nothing is actually necessary, nothing needs to be fought about or protected.

Second, the realisation that nothing in our religion is actually necessary for us to live a spiritual life is an immensely liberating thing. For many people, religion is not an asset which enables them, but a burden which they carry around. It does nothing for them, and they feel guilty that it does nothing for them. Some people give it up, but others just plod on under the impression that, like a nasty tasting medicine, it must somehow be doing them good. When religion is like an ill-fitting garment it restricts our every movement and we die a little every day. To realise that religion is not necessary to our spiritual life can, for some people, feel like being let out of prison. Jesus said:

> He has sent me to proclaim release to the captives and recovery of sight to the blind, to let the oppressed go free, to proclaim the year of the Lord's favour.[8]

Jesus, the man who sat lightly to religious practice, proclaimed that "the Sabbath was made for man, not man for the Sabbath." So many of the laws and customs of his day he overturned, putting the need of the individual above ritual practice. Jesus was supremely indifferent to religion; not that he did not care about it, but that he was unattached to it, and this is the great secret of a healthy religious

8. Luke 4:18-19

belief.

Although nothing is necessary in religion, as I have said above, we may choose to practice religion as part of our spiritual life. Most of us like to have aids and reminders in many areas of living, this is no less true with spirituality. If we choose a religion to aid us that is fine, as long as we do not become too attached to it. For as soon as we become attached it ceases to be an aid and starts becoming an anchor. To have a healthy disinterest in our religion means that we keep the focus on becoming spiritually alive.

On more than one occasion when people have to talk with me about their spiritual life, I have suggest that they stop doing something that is very central to them. It may be to stop reading the Bible for a period of time, or to stop praying in a particular way. The initial response is always one of slight bemusement, but it has, without fail, enabled that person to move on from their position in a way that has enabled their spiritual growth. We cling onto our habits and beliefs as though they are a life-line, yet so often they turn out to be the cords that bind us.

My wife who works in mime and physical theatre (a woman of many parts), described to me a performance that she had seen by a famous French Company. A man enters the stage holding a briefcase. He is attached at the back to ropes which restrict his movements. On the far side of the stage, hanging on a piece of string, is a pair of scissors. The man labours to get across the stage; several times he almost reaches the scissors but is pulled back just before he gets there. Everybody in the audience is willing him to reach the scissors. If only he can get there he can cut himself free. Eventually, triumphantly, he reaches the scissors, snips them free from the string that holds them. At last he can release himself and be free! Instead, he opens his briefcase to reveal a collection of scissors, adds the new pair, and is then dragged off stage by the ropes.

Religion used aright sets us free to be ourselves and enables us to live a life of love and care with those around us. Religious practice, when we are too attached to it, alienates us from our fellow travellers, narrows our vision, and prevents us from living a life of freedom which is our right and duty as human beings.

Nothing in my religion is necessary, nothing in your religion is necessary. What we choose to practise, we choose to practise because we want to, and if we do not want to, then we had better do some serious thinking about our motivation. Is it fear, habit, or indoctrination?

Be religious by all means, but do it because you want to, do it because it is helpful, and do it in the knowledge that no other living soul has to, or ought to, do in the same way as you.

CHAPTER 13
There's None So Queer As Folk

That lovely old Yorkshire (I think) saying that: "All worlds queer 'cept thee and me, and I'm no so sure about thee" puts quite nicely the way we often feel about other people. Why can't others see things the way I do? Part of the answer is to do with psychological type. What do I mean by this, and why does a book on 'secular spirituality' need to delve into psychology?

Psychological type is a way of understanding why people are different from each other. In any group of people, it soon becomes obvious that there are some very basic differences in the way each person approaches life. There are the laid-back types who let the world roll by. The frantic, must organize everything down to the last second, types. The hail-fellow-well-met types who are the life and soul of every gathering. Or there is the shy and reserved type who will say little and have to be drawn into every conversation by someone else.

The difference in the way people 'see' the world, and interact with it, can either be positive to a relationship or situation, or potentially very destructive. Our spiritual journey is about living life to the full for ourselves, and enabling others to do the same. An understanding of our, and other people's psychological type, can be one of our many aids on the spiritual journey. It is one way of making sense of our reactions in any given circumstance, and helps us to understand where others are 'coming from'.

The Swiss psychiatrist and psychotherapist Carl Jung made a study of different types of people, and of the way each type interacted with the world at large and with other individuals. This work was then taken further by Isabel Myers who, with her mother, Katharine Briggs developed a psychological 'test' (test is not really the best name to give, as preference rather than ability is measured), which indicates a person's preference on a sixteen point scale. It is not my intention to go into any depth on this subject because to do so would require a book in itself. However, I do think that it is worthwhile giving a brief outline of psychological type because it is so crucial in the way we relate to those around us.

In the first chapter of this book I recounted the story of my dismal failure to identify the right person on a video presentation of a street crime. Part of this failure I put down to my not being a 'sensing' person. Until I went on a Myers-Briggs Type Indicator (MBTI) weekend, I really had little idea that different types of people really do perceive the world in very different ways, yet this is clearly the case. It is helpful to know and understand this type difference when encountering somebody who just cannot 'see' what I 'see', or when I cannot 'see' what they 'see'. Let's use an example.

My wife and I were married for quite a number of years before we both, at different times, went to an MBTI weekend. In all of those previous years, our holidays were always something of a contentious issue. I like to relax with a pile of books (which I may or may not read) and do very little. For me, holiday is about space to do nothing. Ruth on the other hand, likes to be up and doing. Sports, walks, exploration, visiting; For her, holiday is about re-charging her batteries by engaging in activity with a lot of external stimulus. Holidays always ended up as a compromise that neither of us was really happy with. Either I would be feeling worn-out by too much activity, or Ruth would be feeling bored by our inertia.

Does this ring bells with you? Holidays are often a family nightmare, rather than the time of refreshment and enjoyment that they are meant to be. Why? Because different psychological types require different ways of being refreshed. Ruth's ideal is my nightmare, and vice-versa. Having both completed a MBTI weekend, we found that out of the four scales, we were different on one, the introvert-extravert scale.

Carl Jung introduced the words introvert and extravert into

our language, and they are now used to indicate that someone is either shy and retiring (introvert), or boisterous and gregarious (extravert). Often the former is thought of in rather negative terms, whilst the latter has more positive connotations. In fact, in Jung's original definition, neither is better or worse than the other. With all of the sixteen different types developed in the MBTI, no value judgement is made. Our psychological preference can be likened to whether or nor we are left or right handed. At a push, we can use our other hand, and probably with practise, would become quite proficient. But we prefer one hand to the other.

To be an introverted type means that a person prefers to spend their energies on internal rather than external issues. Ideas and concepts are more important than outside activity. Introverts are more likely to want to think everything through before uttering a word, and are usually quite happy with their own company, or in the company of just a few other people well known to them. They will require their own space and a certain amount of 'peace and quiet'. If this is not available, introverts are likely to become worn out and function less well. To re-charge their batteries, introverts will usually need a certain degree of quiet and space where they are not 'taxed' by too much external demand or stimulus.

Extraverts on the other hand prefer to expend their energies on the external world. Action and interaction are vital for the extravert to function properly. Thinking is often done 'out loud' in a constant stream, 'bouncing ideas' off those around in order to develop their thought processes. Extraverts will usually be happy in the company of a lot of people (but not always), and breadth of social contact will be favoured over depth. Being alone is not something an extravert would want much of, generally preferring to be in company. To re-charge the batteries, an extravert will want to interact with the environment in an active way, external stimulus is the very stuff of life for the extravert.

Knowing this about one another does not instantly make for

easy holidays for Ruth and myself, but we are now aware of each other's needs, and can build it into the programme. We can give ourselves the space and permission to do our own activities (or none), without feeling that somehow our marriage is lacking because our needs are different. Knowing about psychological type doesn't change the reality, but understanding it prevents the difference becoming a disaster.

Earlier I mentioned my lack of sensing. The second part of the MBTI scale is our preference in the way we perceive the world. Having already said in chapter 1 that perception is a creative process, what this scale does is to indicate in which way our creative processes prefer to function. The perceptive scale is divided between those who are predominantly sensing, and those who prefer intuition. These are two ways of 'seeing', both equally valuable, but each very different from the other.

The person who favours sensing as their perceptive process is very much set in the here and now. They use their five senses, to make sense (literally) of their surroundings and will interpret reality according to what is actually present. The sensing person will have a good eye for detail, and will probably be able to recall a scene with much greater literal accuracy than an intuitive person. A sensing person is grounded in the present and is good at interpreting the facts as they are, but will not tend to be as good at seeing other possibilities.

The intuitive person will tend to be far less noticing of concrete reality, sometimes missing what is 'on the end of their nose'. The strength of the intuitive lies in seeing possibilities and implications. Their concentration is not on what is in the present, but in the future, on where this might lead, or what the probable outcome might be. Intuitives tend to be good 'ideas' people, creative and imaginative, but might not be so good at actually getting things done.

Some months ago, whilst I was driving to Oxford on the motorway, my mind was way ahead of my self. Where will I park?

How many roundabouts do I need to negotiate? Will I arrive on time? I was using my preferred function of intuition allowing the sensing part of me to take a back seat. As a result I completely failed to see the sign, huge as it is, and missed the turn-off for Oxford. I had to do a very large detour to get to my destination, only just on time.

It is easy when working or living with someone who perceives the world differently from us, to feel that they are just being awkward. The sensor might think "Why on earth can't she just stick to the facts", whilst the intuitive person would be thinking "Can't he see what will happen if we do it this way?". It can be a recipe for disaster and discord, of argument and loggerhead. Yet it need not be so. Both functions are as vital as one another.

When people of different perceptual orientations understand about psychological type, they see their opposite number not as a threat, but as somebody who will complement and enable the process in which they are involved. It could be in a marriage, or at work, in school (a child who perceives differently from her or his teacher might be in serious trouble if the teacher is not aware of type difference), or in our leisure activities. Committee meetings (PTA, Scouts, Church, Residents Assoc., Bowling Club... you name it) are usually fraught with people being at odds with one another. When we begin to grasp the implication of psychological type difference, the possibility for constructive dialogue and increased cooperation becomes enormous.

The third category in the MBTI scale is about the way we judge or organise the world. It is to do with the way that we come to conclusions. Having perceived the world in a particular way, we then handle that information in two quite different ways. In the MBTI they are called thinking and feeling. As with the categories above, we all have and make use of both functions, we simply prefer one to the other. To be a thinker does not mean that you have no feelings, nor does it mean that feeling people cannot use their brains.

Those whose preferred way of organising the world is thinking, tend to be logical and cool headed in their approach. They will look at all the facts and 'balance the books' according to practical and rational principles. The strength of the thinking type is the ability to be analytical and matter-of-fact in decision making according to clear-cut criteria. The weakness is the likelihood of overlooking the human element which can have serious consequences. Bad industrial relations are almost certain to follow decisions made by a solely 'thinking' management team.

Those who prefer to organise or judge their world through feelings do so with the human element in the forefront of their minds. Decisions will be made on how it will affect people. Will they like it? Can they do it? Is it pleasing? etc. The strength of this approach is that people are likely to be carried with you and there will be a sensitivity to the needs of those involved. The weakness is that the basic facts might be ignored. A management team made up of all 'feelers' would probably have the work force with them - right up to the point when the company goes bust.

Again, a good team will consist of people who have both preferences, and they will value each other for the insights that each can bring to the other.

I heard a story of a hospital that needed to close some of its wards. One plan put forward was to close a maternity ward and combine it with a gynaecological word. On paper this seemed an obvious choice. All the evidence of location, specialisation, equipment usage etc. pointed to it being the 'perfect' solution. My guess is that all those involved in that decision were 'thinkers'. The facts pointed to it, so the choice was obvious.

Had there been a fair representation of 'feelers' on the committee making the decision, they would probably have pointed out the inhumanity of placing women who had miscarried or who had needed an abortion next to those with healthy babies, or perhaps even more painfully, next to a woman having suffered a still-birth. Thinking and feeling need one another for a balanced and truly spiritual life style.

The three sets of categories above are those that Carl Jung worked on and studied. Isabel Myers added a fourth category which indicates which out of the perceiving options (sensing - intuition) and of the judging options (thinking - feeling) is shown most fully to the outside world. If a person is strongest on perception, rather than judging, and his preference is sensing, then this is the element of his psychological type that will be most evident to those around him. If on the other hand a person is stronger on judging, and her preference is feeling, then feeling is what those around her will be most aware of.

At the end of an MBTI workshop one is presented with a set of letters which represents your most likely preferred psychological type. The four polarity scales are:

1. Extravert (E) Introvert (I)
2. Sensing (S) Intuitive (N)
3. Thinking (T) Feeling   (F)
4. Judging (J) Perceiving (P)

From the four scales comes a possibility of sixteen combinations; each type is written up to give a brief summary of what preferences each psychological type has, and the way in which they interact with the world. When I first read mine, it was like reading my autobiography.

Part of the spiritual journey, as I have said above, is about knowing ourselves. The MBTI is a useful indicator of psychological type and can be a big help in enabling us to be more aware of who we are, with all our strengths and weaknesses, needs and gifts. Our psychological type colours all that we are and do. I am an I.N.F.P. Perhaps you will recognise my type in the biases that are bound to be present in this book.

In one short chapter I can do no more than scrape the surface of psychological type. For those who are attempting to live a spiritual life, a life of positive interaction with others, it is important that we at least realise the concept of psychological type, even if we do not wish to go into further detail. Much of who we are, and consequently, the decisions we make is affected by our own type, and by the type of those with whom we have to deal in life. A spiritual life is a life lived to the full, to its greatest potential, knowledge of what makes ourselves and others 'tick' can greatly enhance the process. A little knowledge may be a dangerous thing, but no knowledge at all can be disastrous.

PART TWO

CHAPTER 14
Do you feel myth-understood?

Do you feel myth-understood? No, this is not part of my dyslexia, I really mean it. Being myth-understood is something that happens to me quite a lot. In our rational and scientific age, where truth is portrayed as objective, factual, historical and concrete we have lost the ability to recognise truth when presented in less tangible terms. At least, this seems to be true for certain areas of life.

In chapter ten I used the famous line from Robbie Burns to illustrate that metaphor is still very much part of our current language. "My love is like a red, red rose" still resonates within the heart of anyone who has been, or is, in love. To argue that it isn't true, i.e. that my love does not have a prickly stem, green leaves and a petalled head would not even enter into most people's thoughts. In matters of the heart, where erotic love is concerned, analogy and poetry are quite acceptable.

Once we move away from that realm of experience however, something seems to click in people's brains and the twentieth century rationalist takes over. Yet as I have argued in previous chapters, the most important area of human living, that which gives meaning to life, does not lie in the realm of objective observable matter, but in the cojective experience. The meaninglessness which so many people experience comes precisely from the fact that they are not in relationship; not with themselves, not with others, nor with their environment.

When there is a lack of cojective interrelation, people feel like objects with no personal worth. Their behaviour patterns then reflect this belief either in anti-social activities, and/or in neurotic or psychotic symptoms. In debunking religion, superstition, lores and fables, our modern scientific age has thrown the baby out with the bath water.

In bygone ages many myths were believed to be historically and literally true; it is quite right that, as scientific knowledge increased, we should no longer try to hang on to the literal interpretations of a previous age. But to discard the story altogether is perhaps even more foolish.

It is not that in modern times we don't enjoy a good story; we certainly do. Despite television and video, a good film will still attract large audiences at cinemas. The reason that some films are so successful is because they touch that point of the human consciousness which is alive to the cojective. The incredibly successful Star Wars trilogy was not only technically brilliant, but it carried within it the myth of our humanity; the fight between the dark side of ourselves and the spiritual side. Hook, again, was a technical masterpiece, but it also touched very deeply on the issue of the importance of relationships over against power and material prosperity.

In the film Jurassic Park, like those mentioned above, the special effects were quite astonishing; yet beyond the sheer spectacle and excitement was the underlying theme of humankind out of relationship with creation. I do not think it is an exaggeration to call it prophetic, for it fires a warning shot across the bows of those who would have no restrictions on genetic science and experimentation.

The great difference between modern times and past ages is not that we do not enjoy a good story any more, but that we dismiss it as just that, a good story and nothing more. Before the Enlightenment of the Eighteenth century, when rational and scientific knowledge become the order of the day, people believed the myths of the bible to be literally true; as increasing knowledge proved this not to be the case, the power of the story was lost because it did not match up to scientific accuracy. From that point until this present day the Church has been fighting a rearguard action, slowly admitting that some things are not literally true after all.

First it was the creation stories in Genesis. To start with it was regarded as absolute heresy to question the literal truth of the Garden of Eden story. Of course there was a talking snake in the garden tempting Eve with an apple; it was the word of God! Now, the proportion of Christians who believe this story literally is relatively small. Yesterday's heresy becomes today's orthodoxy. But the Church is slow to adapt and admit that in the past it may not have been right about things.

I was interested to read that it took the Roman Catholic Church over three hundred and fifty years to admit officially that it was wrong to brand Galileo a heretic for saying that the earth was not the centre of the universe. Even then it took a Vatican enquiry lasting several years to come to that conclusion.

Within the Church there seems to be a general reluctance to take myth seriously. 'Truth' for the majority of people, including most Christians, has come to mean that which is objectively and literally true. The word 'myth' is defined by the majority of people as 'a story which is not true'.

When, in 1977 a group of theologians published a book called *The Myth of God Incarnate*, all hell broke loose. Many people, some of whom I suspect had never even read the book, basically accused them of saying that the story of Jesus was not true. This stubborn insistence that truth is only to be found in literal and objective interpretation is not only naive, as history has demonstrated only too well, but it denies the most fundamentally important aspect about humanity; namely that meaning lies in the cojective relationship, and not in objective criteria.

A story which is a myth may or may not have any literal accuracy in it. It may or may not have actually happened at some point in history. What it is vital to grasp is that neither is important in itself. In actual fact it may be more important to realise that a myth is not literally true in order to be able properly to understand it.

What, after all does "my love is like a red, red rose" mean if taken literally? It becomes a nonsense. Likewise, many of the biblical stories, if simply taken at their face value, lose their original meaning. Let's look at a good old favourite.

> So they picked Jonah up and threw him into the sea; and the sea ceased from its raging. Then the men feared the Lord even more, and they offered a sacrifice to the Lord and made vows. But the Lord provided a large fish to swallow up Jonah; and Jonah was in the belly of the fish three days and three nights.[9]

If I had a pound for every time that I have heard the literal truth of this story debated, I would be a wealthier man. Because people get stuck on this one detail, the whole point of the story is missed. Historically, there never was a man named Jonah; at least not this particular Jonah. The story was written by an unknown author at a time when the people of Israel were being particularly exclusive in their attitudes. They held the view that they were the only people whom God cared about; everyone else was 'beyond the pale'. The point of the story had nothing to do with the 'big fish', but rather is contained at the end of the story where God shows mercy to Nineveh. This myth or parable was written for no other reason than to make the point to the readers that God's love was greater than their exclusive behaviour.

To get caught up in whether or not it actually happened at a time and place in history, is like trying to identify the spot on the road where the Good Samaritan rescued the traveller.

MYTH IS A STORY WHICH CONVEYS A SPIRITUAL TRUTH - IT IS A STORY ABOUT YOU AND ME; NOT TO BE BELIEVED IN, BUT TO BE LIVED OUT.

Myth is concerned with cojective experience, with what gives meaning to life; it is concerned about our relationships and

9. Jonah 1:15-17

122

with what makes life worth living.

Myth is true, not because it actually happened at some time in the past, but because it encapsulates the true nature of what it means to be a human being, with all our hopes and fears, joys and sorrows, successes and failures. In many ways myth is more true than concrete fact.

Myth is concerned with what it means to know and be known as a person; objective fact is to do with knowing about and being known about; the difference is one of quality.

Many people today, in increasing numbers, are giving up on religion. I am not surprised. Not only can the liturgy (formal worship) be extremely tedious and long-winded, but the words of the service, and the sermons too, give the impression that to be a Christian means believing in fairy stories. Children are often part of the Church until they start to think critically. At that time there is a whole package which gets thrown out. When Father Christmas and fairies get the big heave-ho, so do the virgin birth and angels. They are understood in much the same light, and are seen to have just about the same amount of relevance in a technological age.

This is a pity; the myths of the Christian tradition, as the myths of the other great religions, hold within them some eternal truths. We do not have to jettison the whole package, we simply have to realise what is the nature of the beast we are dealing with. In its very inadequate way, religion holds a storehouse of treasures; its myths speak to us, not of some supernatural other world, not of past events long forgotten, nor of some objective moral standard to which we have to conform. The myths of religion speak of the spiritual life, of a quality of being which is about personal relationships, and about being who we have it within us to be.

It is not my intention in this book to try and persuade people back into religion. Institutionalised religion is not for everyone, even at its best, and at its worst it is positively death-dealing to the spiritual life. What I want to emphasise though is this; although the

Church (and other religions as well) has often failed in the past, and continues to fail today, nevertheless, the spiritual truths that lie at its heart, and which are contained in its myths are of constant' and universal application. Myth is your story and my story, and when we enter into it, we are enabled to live that quality of life which is eternal. Like love and art and beauty, myth is understood cojectively not objectively; to reject myth is to deny ourselves a source of wisdom which enables the spiritual traveller.

For those of my fellow Christians who insist that the Bible, or in particular, the New Testament, has to be believed in as literal and historical truth, I want to say this: I do not want to convert you. If your belief enables you to live a life which is full and free and liberating, all to the good. But please, do not insist that your reality is the only reality; it may be for you, and that is fine, but it is not for me, and it is also not for millions of other people.

Please reflect on history; the Church has tortured and killed for the sake of so called 'objective beliefs', subsequently proved wrong. Please understand; myth is not a denial of the truth, it is the highest form of truth which objective facts alone can never convey.

In the following chapters I will be regarding the Gospels, Matthew, Mark, Luke and John as myth. In doing this I am not denying that Jesus actually lived, nor that he was put to death by crucifixion; these things are as factual as anything else in ancient history. Nor am I denying that many of the reported incidents actually happened. Myth does not necessarily deny historicity, what it does do is to say that regardless of how much is history or not, there is a truth here which is greater than objective fact. It is a universal truth about the nature of humanity which transcends the limited and particular occurrences of history.

CHAPTER 15

Old Book - New Look

As we have seen above, the Bible need not be understood in terms of history and fact alone. The real significance of scripture (of whatever religion) is that the relevance of the story remains true for every successive generation. For the first seventeen hundred years since the time of Jesus, the world view remained much the same; the earth was the centre of the universe, heaven was a place above the dome of the sky where God lived, and below the earth was hell. And although during the eighteenth and nineteenth centuries this view was increasingly questioned, it was not until this century, when our scientific knowledge accelerated with astonishing rapidity, that the world view of the Bible no longer fitted into people's understanding of life and the universe.

Increasingly science 'disproved' the Bible; the first cosmonaut proclaimed, having 'been there', that there was no God in heaven - a great triumph for an atheist state. Today's generation, at least in the technologically advanced countries of the world, is so far removed from the understanding of the 1st century Middle East that connections can no longer be made. Yet there is a strand that remains unbroken, and that is the basic nature of humanity itself.

When one reads history and literature it becomes obvious that, although perceptions change with growing knowledge, and the influence of differing cultures interact upon one another, woman and man remain at heart, the same.

Whilst I am highly critical of religion, especially in its institutionalised form, nevertheless there remains at its core a wisdom, a fundamental truth which is ageless, because it expresses the fundamental truths of what it means to be human.

Many people feel that Jesus as a man is someone to whom they can relate, yet the doctrines and creeds that have been built up around him over the centuries have turned him into a figure of disbelief. Every Sunday millions of Christians stand up in church and recite the creed, yet I know for a fact that there are many of them who simply do not believe, at least literally, in what they are saying; and this is true for both lay people and clergy alike. There is a terrible lack of integrity in the Church; it uses language and doctrinal formulations of a bygone time and refuses to accept that we are now living in a very different world. By its insistence on 'orthodox belief' it forces some people either to be untrue to themselves, or simply to vote with their feet and leave the church altogether or not join it in the first place.

Not surprisingly huge numbers of people are opting for the latter course of action. An institution which proclaims that its main agenda is ultimate truth, yet which forces many of its members to live a lie is bound to lose credibility in the end. Yet it need not; as an institution the Church only needs to recognise that it is quite legitimate to have more than one view on the same subject. At the end of the day, it is surely not what people believe that really matters, but how that belief affects their day to day living. When I read the Gospels, I do not get the picture of Jesus as a man who was concerned about people's beliefs, but rather how they lived their lives. Issues of love, compassion, justice and mercy seem to dominate his teaching and life, not matters of belief.

The church has perhaps been on the wrong track since the earliest times, or at the least, getting its priorities wrong. Once the first-hand experience of Jesus and the apostles was lost, then second-hand belief became the order of the day. Jesus was concerned with right living and right relationships (orthopraxis). The Church as an institution has been concerned with the right beliefs about Jesus (orthodoxy). The switch was from first-hand living to second-hand living, or in other words, from spirituality to religion.

The four Gospels were written, not as biographies, not as

objective historical documents, but as a means of proclaiming a message of faith. In understanding the Gospels in a new way for this present generation, I want to get back beyond the religious life of the Church to the spiritual experience of Jesus himself. This I propose to do by examining some of the 'life events' of Jesus in the light of some modern psychological understanding. I have placed 'life events' in inverted commas because I do not wish to get into the argument about whether or not some of these things actually happened. Whether or not they did, or if they did, what form they actually took, need not bother us unduly here. What the stories represent is of far greater importance than their historical accuracy, or lack of it. We are dealing with myth, and, as we have seen above, myth is a story into which we are invited to enter and make it our own.

The significance of these stories is precisely not because they are unique, the recollections of a super-human interloper, but because they represent you and me; they are archetypal of the human condition.

Traditionally the life of Jesus, his teaching, death and resurrection are understood as an act of salvation. The sins of humanity, starting with the 'original sin' of Adam's love for apples through to every other sin committed ever since, is said to be taken away by the death of Jesus on the cross. In fact, that Jesus came from heaven to earth precisely in order to be killed to 'pay the price of sin'. This in itself seems to me a thoroughly good reason for not believing in God.

The idea that any being requires a sacrifice of blood to be made as recompense for being wronged is revolting enough, but to suggest that an all powerful being requires it is literally, beyond belief. Yet it was part of the belief structure of many primitive cultures. Blood sacrifice, be it human or animal, was thought necessary to placate the deity. Animal sacrifice was part of Jewish ritual at the time of Jesus, and so no wonder that his death was interpreted in this way.

But we have moved on since then, we have indoor plumbing now, microwaves and televisions, computers and aeroplanes. Our world is nothing like the world of first century Palestine, so why on earth should our beliefs remain the same?

The life of Jesus was interpreted by people of his time for people of his time, but what may have been good enough for Saint Paul is definitely not good enough for us. If the life of Jesus is to mean anything at all to those of us living at the end of the twentieth century, and in a highly sophisticated technological age, then it requires reinterpreting in a language of this present time. To understand Jesus in contemporary society we need not to strip away the myth, for myth is the essential medium in which truth is contained, but rather to create new myths for a new age. Jesus himself said it, yet the Church seems hell bent on ignoring it.

> No one sews a piece of unshrunk cloth on an
> old cloak, for the patch pulls away from the cloak,
> and a worse tear is made. Neither is new wine put
> into old wineskins; otherwise, the skins burst, and the
> wine is spilled, and the skins are destroyed; new wine
> is put into fresh wineskins, and so both are preserved.[10]

Jesus's teaching and his whole way of living demands a new response in every age. To continue to understand Jesus in the light of first century theology is indeed to put new wine into old wineskins; as a consequence both are ruined and the message of one of the world's great human beings becomes distorted and made 'undrinkable'. The 'new wineskins' of psychology is a way of putting into modern terms the eternal truths lived out and taught by Jesus.

I realise that what I am suggesting in the following pages will not appeal to everyone. It is not meant to. What I am most concerned with are two things. First, that the wisdom and truth enshrined in

10. Matthew 9:16-17

the person of Jesus is not lost to a modern age because of its packaging. Second, that there is a way of affirming the life of Jesus and all that he stood for, without the necessity for compromising one's integrity by pretending to subscribe to beliefs that are untenable in a modern society.

In the chapters which follow we shall be looking at five 'events' in the life of Jesus. These are: Birth and Beginnings, Wilderness, Transfiguration, Death and Resurrection and Ascension. By looking at these 'events' from a psychological perspective it is possible to bring them into our own time and understand them as a model for our own spiritual journey. That is not to say that we should attempt to emulate Jesus. This is one of the biggest mistakes of the Church. We are not meant to be like Christ, but rather to be Christ-like. This is not just a question of words and being a nit-picker, but is of vital importance. To be like Christ is to try and copy somebody else, and this is to live a second-hand life. To be Christ-like on the other hand is to be like him inasmuch as he was fully and authentically himself. This is what the message of Jesus is all about; authentic living, being ourselves and, in being fully ourselves, being able to relate in a fully meaningful way with others.

In seeing Jesus in this way, as a model for our own full humanity, Christianity comes alive in a way that it never can when Jesus is understood as being of quite a different order from us. As Son of God he is a figure from history to be believed in or not, as the case may be, and as I have said before, history shows that belief, in itself, does not necessarily alter people's behaviour for the better. But as a human being who lived his life to the full, as a person who gives us a flavour of what we have it in us to become, then we are challenged to live life like that too.

Here we have reached the heart of what being a spiritual person is all about. It is not about believing certain things, nor is it emulating someone else's life, no matter how worthy they might be, nor is it being religious. What it is quite simply, is to live one's life authentically; to be fully and truly who you are, no more and no less. Jesus offers us a model for this, a model which enables us to enter into that quality of living which is divine, known in the Gospels as the Kingdom of Heaven; it is life lived with the quality of eternity.

A saint who lived in the second century, Irenaeus, summed up in a few words the nature of spirituality, thus: "The glory of God is a human being who is fully alive."

However we conceive God, or indeed whether we conceive of God existing at all in conventional theistic terms does not really matter. A human being who is fully alive is what we aim to be, it is the goal of the spiritual journey. If looking at the life of Jesus from a psychological perspective enhances this goal for you, then all to the good; if it does not, then forget it. The vital thing is that we enter into the myth so that it transforms us and enables us to live out our own potential. Each person will need to do this in her or his own unique way, finding the truth that will 'ring bells' and resonate to their own inner truth. The poet Robert Browning in *Paracelsus* expresses it nicely:

> There is an inmost centre in us all,
> Where truth abides in fullness; and around,
> Wall upon wall, the gross flesh hems it in,
> This perfect clear perception - which is truth... and to know,
> Rather consists in opening out a way
> Whence the imprisoned splendour may escape,
> Than in effecting entry for a light supposed to be without.

The language of psychology is one way in which modern humanity can once again enter into the myth and find ancient truths resonating with contemporary ideas. To allow this to happen is to have one's perception changed, to be 'born again', which takes us on to the first 'life event' of Jesus; Birth and Beginnings.

CHAPTER 16
Birth and Beginnings

The first event for us to consider is the birth of Jesus. Two of the four Gospels recount the nativity story - virgin birth, angels, shepherds, wise men etc.; the other two do not mention it. For me this is a good indication that we are not talking about history, but story. If such facts as a virgin birth were actually known about, one would expect it to have been an important part of the message from the beginning. As it is, only half the Gospels record it, and it is conspicuous by its absence from the letters of Saint Paul, which are the earliest writings of the Church.

Yet the stories of the virgin birth are not to be dismissed out of hand; along with other material they point to an important psychological truth; that is, that our birth is not simply a once only physical experience, but is a continuing psychological process.

In the prologue to the fourth Gospel, Saint John writes this:

But to all who received him, who believed in his name, he gave power to become children of God, who were born, not of blood or of the will of the flesh or of the will of man, but of God.[11]

Being born "not of blood or of the will of the flesh or of the will of man, but of God" sounds like another description of a virgin birth. But here, the writer is not talking about the birth of Jesus, but of every Christian believer. The spiritual truth which is embedded in the nativity stories is made more explicit by John. Jesus's 'virgin birth' is a model for our own spiritual birth, and it is a theme which continues throughout the Gospels.

In a very real way each of us has two births. We are born as physical creatures, but we are also spiritual and psychological beings

11. John 1:12-13

131

as well. Our progress to physical maturity is, on the whole a steady one, and is complete within the first twenty years or so. Our psychological and spiritual growth is far less guaranteed however, and will depend very largely upon our interactions with others.

Psychological birth is a process rather than an event, one which we can be increasingly open to, or one which we close off and shut down. To speak of a virgin birth is to talk spiritually or psychologically, not literally and physically. Someone who is 'born of a virgin' is a woman or man who is spiritually and psychologically open and alive; it is to speak of the quality of their present state of being, rather than referring back to an actual physical event.

It is easy for us to forget, reading the Gospels as we do, that the life and teaching of Jesus came first; the stories about Jesus came later, and a good many years later at that. Jesus's teaching had a lot to say about being psychologically open, but naturally, he used the language of his day not ours. He spoke of being "born again", and of the need to become like little children.

These are profound insights into psychological and spiritual well being and, as such, are as true today as they were when he first uttered them.

When our daughter Freya was quite small and just beginning to learn a basic vocabulary, she made the type of mistake that every child does at that stage. Living near to the Thames, we used quite often to go and feed the ducks. At first everything that splashed around and ate the bread was "duck". After a while she began to discriminate between ducks, coots, geese etc. This is the process which the Swiss psychologist Jean Piaget called assimilation and accommodation. At first, Freya had a very basic frame of reference; in this case it was that all animals with wings that swam and ate bread were "duck". Any new breed that happened along was assimilated into her single "duck" category. Put simply, assimilation is a process by which we bend the facts to fit what we already know. As children grow and their experience and knowledge expands, so they learn to accommodate. In learning to distinguish between ducks, coots and geese, Freya altered her own frame of reference to accommodate external facts rather than 'bending' them.

This process of first assimilating facts, followed by accommodating to the facts, is the continual process of childhood. In a sense it is a constant willingness to be proved wrong, learn something new and move on. Although children can seem stubborn in the face of facts that they cannot yet accommodate, it is not true stubbornness, but rather a frustration at being given facts which are as yet beyond their grasp. Once children have reached the stage to understand, they are only too willing to accommodate.

Psychologically there is a constant process of re-birth going on in children. Every time they are able to let go of a wrongly assimilated piece of information, and accommodate their thinking to match the reality, they have, in a small way been 'born again'.

At that time the disciples came to Jesus and asked, "Who is the greatest in the kingdom of heaven?" He called a child, whom he put among them, and said, "Truly I tell you, unless you change and become like children, you will never enter the kingdom of heaven. Whoever becomes humble like this child is the greatest in the kingdom of heaven.[12]

This saying of Jesus has, all too often, been interpreted to mean that to get to heaven (after death) one has to be dependent, meek and subservient. Nothing could be further from what I believe Jesus meant by this. For a start, the kingdom of heaven is a quality of living now, not post mortem. But more importantly, it has nothing to do with being meek and dependent and unable to think for oneself (which is how the Church often treats its members) but has everything to do with the ability and willingness to accommodate

12. Matthew 18:1-4

133

to information rather than assimilate information into already set ideas. Who will be the greatest in the kingdom of heaven? She or he who is willing to keep an open mind - prejudice is not a possibility.

There are two very key words in the passage from Matthew above; change and humble.

To change is to make a conscious decision to be different. It is, in this case, to decide not to pre-judge any situation upon our limited and incomplete knowledge. How hard this is! It means that instead of falling back on comfortable stereotypes we have to assess each situation from scratch, 'with the eyes of a child'. It was this faculty that enabled Jesus to challenge many of the norms and assumptions of his own time; he was alive to the moment and not shackled to the past, he could see what others could not because he looked for possibilities not probabilities. The humility of the child comes from its lack of pride. I know that sounds an obvious statement, but all too often it is the obvious that is easiest to miss.

From where does pride come? It comes surely from feeling that you have 'made it', you have the answers, you have the power, you have the wealth; it is a feeling that in any given area of life you have arrived. The humility of the child comes from just the opposite, in knowing that it has a long way to go, and that it has a great deal more to learn. Change is only possible if we feel the need or desire for it, humility is the knowledge that change is not only desirable, but necessary for full psychological health.

John Henry Newman said: "Here below, to live is to change, and to be perfect is to have changed often."

Failure to be able or willing to change and adapt is an indication that the individual has failed to achieve fully the ability to accommodate. Instead, new facts, new situations are assimilated; they are judged on old criteria which may be totally irrelevant or inaccurate. Such people cause distress to themselves and distress to those with whom they live and work.

No living thing remains unchanged, for anything to remain

unchanging is an indication that life has ceased to be. This is true both organically as well as psychologically and spiritually.

In his encounter with Nicodemus, Jesus was emphatic about what it takes to live his kind of life. Nicodemus starts by talking about the nature of Jesus's life, Jesus answers by telling him what is required for anybody to "see the kingdom of God".

> Now there was a Pharisee named Nicodemus, a leader of the Jews. He came to Jesus by night and said to him, "Rabbi, we know that you are a teacher who has come from God; for no one can do these signs that you do apart from the presence of God." Jesus answered him, "Very truly, I tell you, no one can see the kingdom of God without being born from above." Nicodemus said to him, "How can anyone be born after having grown old? Can he enter a second time into the mother's womb and be born?" Jesus answered, "Very truly, I tell you, no one can enter the kingdom of God without being born of water and spirit. What is born of the flesh is flesh, and what is born of the Spirit is spirit. Do not be astonished that I have said to you, 'You must be born from above.' The wind blows where it chooses, and you hear the sound of it, but you do not know where it comes from or where it goes. So it is with everyone who is born of the Spirit".[13]

From what Jesus is saying it would seem that everyone who is born of the Spirit is unpredictable, you neither know where they are coming from, nor where they are going.

This is just the case with the person who has got into the habit of accommodating. Because people who accommodate are willing to change their perceptions according to circumstances, it means that they cannot be expected to produce the same answers

13. John 3:1-8

every time. You do not know where they are coming from because they do not have fixed criteria into which they assimilate information; you do not know where they are going because the process of accommodation is a creative one which will produce unique reactions.

It is an unfortunate fact that most adults seem to think that they have done sufficient accommodating by the time they reach their early twenties. Of course no one stops altogether, but the process is reduced drastically, and new information is assimilated into already formulated ideas. The old saying that 'there's none so blind as them that won't see' is typical of the assimilator. Life becomes limited and narrow, not because of any external circumstances, but because perceptions becomes set and immovable. The spiritual life is a life that is to be lived to the full, which entails psychological maturity, and that in turn requires a constant attitude of accommodation.

It has been my experience as a counsellor and as a spiritual director that problems occur when people are unable or unwilling to move on, to adjust to new circumstances. The greater the degree of psychological immobility, the greater is the resulting distress.

Jesus's teaching about being 'born again' does not mean that one needs to have a particular type of Christian experience. Too many born again Christians simply swap one set of values for another, and then go on to assimilate everything into that particular mould. They remain just as narrow as they were before, sometimes even more so, everything being measured by the single criterion of a particular religious perception. Being born again is a conscious decision to change. It is being prepared to return to that state of childhood where everything is provisional and is assessed on its own merits. The spiritual truth of this teaching is eternal. We will never see the kingdom of God; that is, we will never live life with an eternal quality, unless we accept the need for constant accommodation. The need to be 'born again', or 'born of the Spirit'

136

is crucial to the teaching and life of Jesus.

He knew then what modern psychology, counselling and psychotherapy may say differently, but the underlying truth remains. People live dysfunctional lives if they become fixed in their responses to life. The degree of dysfunction will depend upon the level to which a person has become stuck, either in their emotional responses and/or in their thinking. If an individual can be enabled to change, which usually means a change in perception, then what can be experienced is literally a feeling of being 'born again'. It is a liberation from patterns of thought and behaviour which restrict and confine.

The therapeutic process of being 'born again' can be experienced in many different ways. Religion at its best can do it, psychotherapy and counselling can do it, as can entering into a loving relationship with a partner where you feel accepted for the person you really are. Being 'born again' or, in other words, experiencing a 'virgin birth' is a human experience available to us all; it is the way which leads to a life lived out to the full.

The story of Jesus's virgin birth must be taken not in isolation, but in union with his teaching on being born again and on becoming like little children. Whether or not one wishes to believe that it is history, is of much less importance than the realisation that it is the model for our own growth into psychological wholeness.

CHAPTER 17
Wilderness - Finding Our Way"

The story of Jesus in the wilderness appears in three of the four gospels. In Mark's gospel, which is generally accepted to be the earliest, we hear that:

> ...the Spirit immediately drove him out into the wilderness. He was in the wilderness forty days, tempted by Satan; and he was with the wild beasts; and the angels waited on him.[14]

In Matthew and Luke we have the elaborated versions which include specific temptations by the devil. What are we to make of these stories? Do they say anything to us in the latter part of the twentieth century? The idea of a personified devil and ministering angels cuts little ice today, even amongst religious people. For those who give little thought to religious symbolism, they represent yet further evidence that Christians are willing to believe almost anything.

Yet wilderness is a reality. It is a reality in literal terms, that is, that people do choose to go into places of wilderness with the express intention of 'listening to their own inner voice'. It is also a reality psychologically. We all experience wilderness times; times of anguish and distress, times when we are no longer certain about our direction, our relationships, or whether life has any meaning or purpose. Even if life has been generally good to you so far, you will, assuming that you have passed through adolescence, have experienced feelings of wilderness.

In the Bible the theme of wilderness runs through the text like a thread. In chapter three of Genesis, after Adam and Eve have eaten the forbidden fruit they are cast out of the garden into what sounds very much like a wilderness.

14. Mark 1:12-13

Cursed is the ground because of you; in toil you shall eat of it all the days of your life; thorns and thistles it shall bring forth for you; and you shall eat the plants of the field. By the sweat of your face you shall eat bread until you return to the ground, for out of it you were taken; you are dust, and to dust you shall return.[15]

Compared to the 'Garden of Eden', all the world is a wilderness in which we have to work hard to find our place. Mostly the garden of Eden story is regarded as depicting the onset of evil brought about by humanity's disobedience to God's will. (It is interesting to see how the man blames the woman, and the women blames the serpent; the art of passing the buck goes back a long way. But the real culprit of this story is God, who expects Eve to know the difference between good and evil before she has eaten of the fruit of that particular tree).

A more positive interpretation of the Genesis Myth is seeing it as representing humanity's journey from the innocence of childhood, through the rebellion of adolescence to the maturity of adulthood. Generally speaking, girls do mature into women earlier than boys into men, so that the picture of Eve leading the way out of childlike innocence into the wilderness of early adulthood is, in fact, a true representation of what actually happens both physically and psychologically.

One cannot speak universally about the experience of adolescence because different cultures have differing traditions and rites of passage. In general terms though, it can be regarded as that period of time, somewhere between early teens and mid twenties, where the body chemistry starts to change, sex becomes of enormous importance, questions of identity and belonging come to the fore. Turmoil, to a greater or lesser degree, takes the place of the relatively calm childhood years which went before (this is not

15. Genesis 3:17-19

to say that childhood years are necessarily good or happy; external circumstances may well prevent this, but there is less internal conflict during this period). Adolescence is truly a time of wilderness, out of which our adult identity is forged.

As King Lear says to his daughter Cordelia, "nothing will come of nothing". Our adult identity is not just given as a gift, out of the blue so to speak, but comes from the complex integration of our inherited genes, our nurture (or lack of it) as infants and children, and our interaction with the world in which we live.

Out of the wilderness of our adolescence comes the basic material of our maturity. The young adult we become will depend very much on the extent to which we have been able and enabled, to work successfully through the difficult issues facing us in adolescence.

Being a parent to an adolescent is one of the most difficult tasks for anyone to manage. Getting the right balance between being supportive and allowing freedom on the one hand, and challenging destructive behaviour and presenting boundaries on the other is an almost impossible line to tread successfully. Sometimes we, as parents or responsible adults will get it wrong; we'll be over protective or too liberal, we'll be seen as authoritarian or uncaring, and the struggle of the young adults with whom we share our lives will re-awaken in us struggles that were not worked through in our own adolescence.

Becoming an integrated personality not only involves the wilderness period of adolescence, but the continual process of facing both in the external world, and in the world of our own inner psyche, times of challenge and testing. The important issue here is to recognise that wilderness is part of our human experience. We cannot completely avoid it, it is part of the fabric of being human, being a person rather than an object. This being the case, it is important that we try and make our times of wilderness into creative rather than destructive experiences. This is done, not by denying or repressing our times of desolation, but by looking them squarely in the face, and using them as tools in our growth to full humanity.

Once we recognise that wilderness is part of our everyday existence, albeit in differing degrees at different life stages, the story of Jesus in the wilderness can take on a new relevance which it may not have had before.

Taken at face value, especially in the extended versions of Matthew and Luke, we see someone who is clearly represented as the unique 'Son of God' doing battle with supernatural forces, and being ministered to by equally otherworldly angels. But what happens if, instead, we see Jesus as a representative figure for our own human struggle? The story of the temptations by the devil take on a new perspective; rather than seeing it as a supernatural assault, it can be understood as the wilderness experience of someone wrestling with his own psyche, of trying to choose the right course of action in difficult circumstances.

Does that not ring bells with all of us at some point or points in our own lives?

Surely the three temptations in Luke 4: 1-13 are representations of temptations that each of us has to face. They are choices about materialism, aggrandisement and power. In the first temptation Jesus is told to turn stones into bread to satisfy his hunger. The answer he gives is well known; "One does not live by bread alone". This is both a spiritual and a psychological truth. Human beings are more than just material beings, and we cannot function adequately if our lives consist of nothing more than material satisfaction.

There is a story that: During the last war, in a Nazi extermination camp, there were two huts of women prisoners. Both had very similar conditions, neither had anything like enough food, clothing or warmth provided, and the long term prospects for them all was poor. Yet out of the two groups of prisoners, one group seemed to fare better than the other. This group had amongst its numbers a very old woman, too old and too weak to work, she received no rations. Those others in the hut shared their meagre rations so as to keep her alive. In return, she told them stories about their tradition, their past and their country. She connected them with a purpose and a meaning to life beyond the squalor and degradation of their present existence. Despite having less food than those in the neighbouring hut, these women had a better survival rate.

Human beings cannot 'live by bread alone', if we try to, or are forced to, it will be to our greater impoverishment. Yet it is a question that we repeatedly have to face; in making our priorities it can be all too easy to ignore the deeper demands of our spiritual nature in favour of a quick materialistic fix.

The next two temptations are both to do with self aggrandisement and power. This may sound as though they have nothing to do with the 'ordinary person on the street', but only to those in positions of responsibility and public office. Not a bit of it. Of course those who do hold power in organisations or government have more obvious power, and the temptation to use power for its own sake, and for the sake of inflating the ego is all too real, both in theory and in practice. But it is a temptation that is open to each one of us on a daily basis.

In all our interaction with other people we have the opportunity to exercise a degree of power.

Do we try and make ourselves look better at the expense of someone else?

Do we treat those 'below' us on the social scale as menials not worthy of our notice, or as valued people in their own right?

Do we measure importance in terms of wealth, possessions, power and influence, or does it rest in the value of the individual as a brother or sister in creation? (and not just on the human scale).

If our self (the ego) remains at the centre of our world, then we have failed in our wilderness encounters; the 'devil' has won

143

and we become diminished as human beings.

In times of wilderness our values and norms are challenged.

Wilderness may be forced upon us by a tragic event; by illness, either physical or psychological, by the death of a loved one, by the loss of a job.

Wilderness may even come as the result of a happy occurrence; getting married, having a baby, moving home or obtaining a degree.

Wilderness is that time when our values and norms no longer stand up to the perceived reality of the situation; it is a time for taking stock, re-evaluating and perhaps changing direction.

Wilderness comes in every degree from the major catastrophe to the minor upset; the common factor is that it requires of us a decision about the direction in which our life is going.

For those who are attempting to live a life in the Spirit, wilderness is an opportunity to look at life, and judge it, in terms of values other than those of the prevailing cultural norms. In recent times, the trend has been towards individual selfishness and aggrandisement.

This was epitomised in the Thatcherite 80s where, according to the Lady, society ceased to exist. It would seem that for people caught up in that kind of culture, the answer to all three of the 'Devil's' questions would have been "Oh yes please".

A crisis or traumatic event can stop us in our tracks and make us look again at such values, to understand that "One does not live by bread alone." But wilderness needs to be more than a series of events which may or may not happen to us during the course of our lives. If we are serious about living a spiritual life, wilderness must be something that we purposely incorporate into our regular activities. Wilderness is an attitude towards life which prevents us from sitting comfortably with the status quo, and challenges us to reassess our priorities and the direction in which we are going.

Many people today choose to do this through the medium of a retreat. This might be religious or non-religious in nature. Some retreats are led, with addresses given on a particular theme to a number of people gathered together, some are individually led with no common input, and yet others simply choose to take themselves away to a quiet spot for a few days (into the wilderness) to think life through at a deeper level than is usually possible.

Whatever may or may not have actually happened to Jesus, I am sure that he would have experienced, on more than one occasion, going into the wilderness. In his place of birth it was quite possible to be in the wilderness, literally as well as metaphorically. It would have been part of his life to search out the truth within his own soul, and then to act upon the answers.

What we have in the wilderness stories related in the gospels is a paradigm for our own spiritual journey. We too will have to contend with the 'devils' of greed, materialism, aggrandisement and power.

To gain from these stories we do not need to believe in them literally. They speak metaphorically of our own need for the discipline of the wilderness experience in our lives, and the need to use creatively those times of wilderness that are thrust upon us against our will or reason. The 'devil' is an ever present tempter within our own psyche who will constantly bid us to take the easy option and live less than fully human lives.

Like men and women who had gone before him, and lived after him, Jesus was a person of supreme integrity, willing to risk his life and go to his death, rather than compromise the truth for which he stood. We are challenged by his life, and by the lives of other great men and women to reach for this level of integrity and truth; but it is a life that is only achieved by the willingness to face our own personal wilderness. Nothing comes from nothing; wilderness cannot be avoided on the road to spiritual and human maturity, the story of Jesus in the wilderness is also our story.

On the bright side, Jesus is, we are told, ministered to by angels. When going through the wilderness, either of our own choosing or one that is brought upon us, we do need angels to minister to us. It has been my experience that, when going through wilderness experiences, there have always been angels around to help pick up the pieces.

They are not usually very obvious in their guise. Usually they come in the form of good friends with whom I have shared something of my journey. They are invariably very down to earth, good humoured and lavish with the gin. If you choose to enter into wilderness in a way that will enable and enhance your spiritual development, make sure you have an angel or two around that you can turn to. This is not a journey which we take alone, it is a cojective journey where heart meets heart. And at some point, when the wilderness has transformed your halo into a doughnut and coffee, and your wings into arms that embrace, you will find that you too are being an angel to somebody else. It's all very human and, as such, all very divine.

CHAPTER 18

Transfiguration - On the right path

The transfiguration of Christ is one of the most problematic 'events' recorded in the gospels. It appears in the first three gospels, with Luke giving the fullest account. Let's have a look at it.

> Jesus took with him Peter and John and James, and went up on the mountain to pray. And while he was praying, the appearance of his face changed, and his clothes became dazzling white. Suddenly they saw two men, Moses and Elijah, talking to him. They appeared in glory and were speaking of his departure, which he was about to accomplish at Jerusalem. Now Peter and his companions were weighed down with sleep; but since they had stayed awake, they saw his glory and the two men who stood with him. Just as they were leaving him, Peter said to Jesus, "Master, it is good for us to be here; let us make three dwellings, one for you, one for Moses, and one for Elijah" - not knowing what he said.
>
> While he was saying this, a cloud came and overshadowed them; and they were terrified as they entered the cloud. Then from the cloud came a voice that said, "This is my Son, my Chosen; listen to him!"[16]

What are we to make of this? Some people suggest that it is a resurrection story which has become 'misplaced' in the text of the gospels. Others would say that it is a myth, a story inserted to make a theological point about Jesus and who he was. Yet others would want to insist that it is simply an account of what actually happened on a mountain in Judea.

16. Luke 9:28-35

Whatever the truth of, or behind the story (and it may be a composite of all three things) we shall never know exactly, but that should not worry us. Our concern here is not historical accuracy or theological correctness, but spiritual reality. What in this story is real for us today? How can we use this story of Jesus as a guide, a marker, in our own journey towards full humanity? For like all of the other biblical stories, and all of the stories and myths of the other great religions, if we do not make them our own in the here and now, they become burdens to weigh us down rather than vehicles for our journey.

I am in my mid-forties, and unless I live into my nineties, I am over halfway through my life. It's all down hill from here. Or is it? There seems no doubt that, in all probability, I now have fewer years left to live than I have already lived; I have passed the halfway mark and the reality of my own mortality, my own death, gets closer with every breath I take. This of course is true from the moment that we are born, but from mid-life onwards it becomes increasingly obvious. My glass is (at least) half empty; or is it perhaps half full? This is a vitally important question because it will determine how I live the rest of my life.

Let's paint a picture that we can identify with. Life is a large glass of wine (or whatever you would like it to be); in the beginning it is full to the top and we drink of it freely because it seems as though it will never run out. As we increase in years however, it becomes clear to us that the wine is decreasing. It is limited and finite after all; how do we react?

One reaction is that of denial. This is quite a popular ploy in modern western society. We pretend that death does not really exist, that the wine will never run out. Death is sanitised, rarely talked about and an embarrassment when encountered. Those who are bereaved often become social outcasts because they are a living reminder that death awaits us all. The bereaved are allowed about two months to 'get over it', after which it is expected that 'normal service will be resumed as soon as possible'. (A normal bereavement period will last anything between two and five years).

The cosmetics industry and plastic surgery thrive on people who are trying to convince themselves that their glass will never empty. Keep looking young, dye your hair, smooth your wrinkles, lift your face. So much time and energy, money and resources goes into denying the onset of old age and death; yet the glass will empty.

Now I am not a kill-joy, I have no problems about people looking good, keeping healthy etc., but taken to extreme, in a vain attempt to deny the inevitable, this simply wastes what time/wine there is left.

What meaning is there in devoting time and energy in trying to avoid the inevitable?

A man builds his house down by the river. It is a beautiful site, and he anticipates spending a long and happy life there. After a while he realises that, over the years, the river has slowly changed its course. His front door, originally thirty feet from the river bank, is now only ten feet away. Rather than face the fact that he will eventually have to give up his house to the river, he starts to reinforce the river bank. Every spare moment he has is taken up with this work, he has time for little else. In old age his efforts could not keep up with the relentlessness of the river. One day, after heavy rainfall, the river burst its banks. He died with his house. There was no one to mourn their loss.

Another reaction to the dwindling amount of wine in the glass is to acknowledge its depletion, and try to conserve what is left. It's the 'I'm too old to do that sort of thing', or the 'I like things as they have always been, thank you very much' approach. Many people, after they reach mid-life, (and sometimes before) avoid the challenge of old age and death by setting their lives in aspic. Change only happens when it is forced upon them from the outside, and then it is resented and resisted. Maintaining the status quo is the name of the game, and it often masquerades under the label of 'old fashioned values' or 'respect for the past'.

Again, there is nothing wrong with either of those things in themselves. There is much good from the past which needs preserving for this, and future generations. But when it is espoused as a foil against the passing of time, an escape into the past which doesn't have to change, then it becomes a denial of life and is as neurotic as the attempt to be forever young. To try and preserve what remains in the glass 'just as it was' is doomed to failure. Not only will the wine eventually evaporate, but in the process it will become sour and undrinkable. Life, like wine, cannot just be preserved, but needs to be used, enjoyed, drained to the dregs.

Draining to the dregs is yet a third way of coping with the half empty glass. Those who, having reached mid-life, recognise that death is an increasingly close visitor, decide to 'drink the glass down'. This is a more admirable reaction to the two alternatives mentioned above, but it tends to place the focus in the wrong place. Life is lived to the full, but almost exclusively at a material level. The sensations are indulged, experiences are sought and energy is expended in the hope that this will give meaning to a limited and finite existence. Such a reaction need not be only self-indulgent.

Great acts of heroism, journeys of adventure and discovery, charitable works; all these can come from a sense of wanting to get to grips with the remainder of life. Much can come of such a reaction to the realisation of our own mortality. Many people will find it a fulfilling experience, whilst others, especially those who have concentrated on their own appetites, will be left feeling empty. The dregs can leave a bitter taste when the wine has been used in excess.

The fourth, and what I want to call the spiritual way, is to realise that the glass is actually never empty. As the level of the wine decreases in the glass, it is not left empty, (nature abhors a vacuum) but is replaced by air (pneuma - spirit). This way of looking at life moves the focus away from quantity, "how much have I got left?" to quality, "what sort of life do I have?".

We are both physical and spiritual beings, but if we live our lives exclusively at the level of the physical and material, "what do I possess? how can I get more? what time is left to me?" then no matter how much we have, we are left wanting more, especially more time. When we recognise the spiritual dimension to our lives, no matter how that may be expressed, we begin to see that the glass is never empty. No matter how much or how little we possess in terms of material wealth, or how much or how little time we have left, our glass is always full. Once one becomes aware that the glass is full, no matter what proportion of wine to air there is, we are set free to get on with life in the here and now. There is no need to try and deny the passage of time, no need to live in the past, and no need to 'eat drink and be merry, for tomorrow we shall die'.

Death is still an unknown, we neither know when it is coming or what, if anything lies on the other side. Neither will death necessarily be a welcome visitor; the spiritual person rejoices in this life. Those who are following a spiritual way in life are able to face the prospect of death without denial because of the quality of their present existence. If life has real meaning, then death is far less to be feared. We need only to acknowledge it, and then get on with what we are doing.

The transfiguration of Jesus seems to me to represent the axis point of life. It is that point in life when we look back over the past, assess the present, and wonder what the future is going to bring.

This is what happens in the story. Jesus meets Moses and Elijah, who represent the Law and the Prophets. Over the period of his ministry, Jesus' teaching was often criticised for not being

151

'orthodox'. Here, in his encounter with Moses and Elijah, he is shown to be vindicated. He, and not the institutions of his time is shown to be the way that leads to God. Jesus' history is compared with the history of Israel, and not found to be wanting.

In the light of this knowledge we are told that "Moses and Elijah... were speaking of his departure, which he was about to accomplish at Jerusalem". The path that Jesus had taken was confirmed to be the right one; his future would continue along in the same direction, which would inevitably lead to his death. The voice from the cloud is yet further confirmation that all is right with this man.

In many works of art, of most religions, holy men and women are depicted as having halos, or as shining with an inner radiance. In my life so far, I have met a couple of people who, if I had to use descriptive language about them, I would say shone. Obviously I do not mean that they literally glowed, but they had something about them that really did seem to 'shine from the inside out'. It is something about a life lived to the full, where choices have been made which lead to that man or woman becoming a fully integrated personality.

The story of the transfiguration of Jesus is just that; the picture of a man who is thoroughly integrated and whole. The pictorial language in which the story is told need not put us off. In its dramatic and other-worldly way it is saying that, in the face of hard choices, in the knowledge and near presence of death, in the face of great opposition, it is still possible to make the right decisions and follow a spiritual path.

At our mid-life point, we may not shine with the glow of complete integration, but neither do we need to despair. Our glass is only half empty if we choose to see it that way. To be transfigured is to see the world from a spiritual perspective, and then live it that way.

In any terms that are understandable from the material point of view, Jesus was an utter failure. He had no recognised power, no wealth, and as far as we know no permanent home. He was killed after just three years of public life, and most of his friends deserted him. I certainly wouldn't make him chief executive of my company! Yet despite such utter failure, his short life changed the world, not because he was magically divine, but because he shows us what it is to be a fully integrated person.

Few people even want to be that whole; instead we get caught up in patterns and behaviours which prevent us from seeing our own potential. Yet there have been, and are, people who have followed his pattern and transfigured, not only themselves, but their world. Saint Francis of Assisi, Mahatma Gandhi and Mother Teresa of Calcutta are but three who spring to mind straight away.

Transfiguration is something we can all experience. It comes from the choices we make, where our priorities lie and the vision we have of life, both our own individual lives, and life in general. It is important therefore that we do not relegate the story of the transfiguration of Jesus to the realms of fairy story, nor should we simply take it as an historical event which did, and could only happen to Jesus.

Transfiguration is that which happens to us when we integrate our lives. When we allow the spiritual to take the place of the material, we are released from the fear of death, and the quality of our lives becomes transformed. But it is not all or nothing. We are not suddenly transfigured into a new being (although profound shifts of perception can lead to a startling change in a person's life).

Becoming transfigured is a process which happens to us as we pursue the spiritual path, a path routed in down-to-earth good sense, love, compassion and a yearning to do the truth.

As I have said before, this type of life may be manifested in and through religion; the three examples above all were or are. Yet it need not be so. We will recognise transfigured lives wherever and however they are lived. We will recognise them, not because of any awareness by them of such a quality within themselves, but because of the effect they have on others, and sometimes, because they really do seem to 'glow' from the inside out.

In the book which he edited entitled *Dying we Live*, H. Kuhn Gollwitzer brought together a collection of letters written by victims of the Nazis. It reveals that, under pressure of death and violence, there were men and women who would rather be imprisoned and killed, than take part in the collective evil which was perpetrated by that regime. Below is just one short extract.

A Farm Boy from the Sudetenland   February 3, 1944.

Dear parents,

I must give you bad news - I have been condemned to death, I and Gustave G. We did not sign up for the SS, and so they condemned us to death. Both of us would rather die than stain our consciences with such deeds of horror. I know what the SS has to do... I thank you for everything you have done for my good since my childhood; forgive me, pray for me...

It is not technology that will be the ultimate saviour of our world, not humankind's manipulation of the environment. Nor will all the pious platitudes of those who place religion at the centre deflect us from heading down the road of chaos and disaster. But what will transform our world will be transfigured lives; lives like that of the Sudetenland Farm Boy.

Each one of us has the choice of how we will live our lives. Being transfigured really is an option for all of us.

In the next chapter we will explore the process by which this can happen.

CHAPTER 19
Death & Resurrection - The process of becoming

The resurrection of Jesus from the dead has been the central proclamation of the Church from its very beginning. It was this 'fact' alone that established the Church and from which the belief that Jesus was the Son of God arose. All of the Church's creeds, doctrines, dogmas, and traditions, all of its institutions and practices, and all that the Church is today stemmed from that one belief, that Jesus rose bodily from the dead.

Yet like the other 'events' in the life of Jesus, there are problems in insisting that the story as recorded in the gospels be taken at face value as literally and historically true.

Try reading all four gospel accounts of the resurrection for yourself.

Who first discovered the empty tomb?

Who were there, angels or men, and how many?

To whom did Jesus first appear, and where?

Was he touched or was he not?

It is quite clear from reading all four stories together that they cannot all be literally true, the 'facts' simply do not add up to one coherent story. Yet we should not be surprised at this. The gospels were not written down until some thirty years and more after the death of Jesus. Stories in the telling and re-telling do get altered.

If you recall my dismal failure to recall events seen by me only minutes before on a television screen, (chapter 1) it is easy to understand how, after over thirty years between the event and its committal to paper, there would be discrepancies between the four texts. What we must admit from this is that we cannot know with any certainty exactly what did or did not happen on that first Easter day. One thing is clear however; to insist that it was Jesus' actual physical body which was re-animated is not consistent with the text. It seems to me that the literal belief in the bodily resurrection of Jesus is no more essential than is the literal belief in the virgin birth.

That is not to dismiss the fact that something must have happened which turned eleven frightened men into bold proclaimers of Jesus' resurrection. It is hard to imagine that any contrived story emanating from the stolen body of a religious leader could have such a dramatic effect.

Nor does the often put theory of Jesus going into a coma on the cross, only to be revived by the cold tomb, cut any ice. Both scenarios presuppose a huge con-trick on the part of both Jesus and/or his followers. Mighty empires come and go, I do not believe it possible that Christianity would have lasted almost two thousand years with nothing more behind it than a cleverly devised religious con!

What I want to challenge is not the resurrection, but the interpretation that was put upon it, and the religious accretions which it has acquired over the centuries.

In chapter 11 I said that I remain agnostic about life after death, and this is so. I cannot know with any certainty whether there is life after death, and, if there is, what form or forms it will take. From the 'evidence' available to me I believe that the probability of life continuing is at least as reasonable as the opposite conclusion. In my agnosticism what I refrain from doing is placing any particular religious interpretation or conclusion on the possibility.

So let us try and look at the resurrection of Jesus, but without the preconceptions of Christianity.

If we look at Jesus of Nazareth as a model, a paradigm for our own full humanity, it is reasonable to assume that what happened to him, is also available to us, not through belief or faith, but by virtue of our shared humanity. One question we can ask is; have any other people, at other times, had what could be called resurrection experiences?

The answer is clearly yes.

In his book *The Silent Road*, Major Tudor Pole recounts this story:

> During the last war a company commander well known to me was killed by a sniper's bullet at the beginning of an engagement in the Palestine hill country. He was so loved by his men that it was decided not to disclose his death until the battle was over. This officer was killed at seven in the morning and yet throughout that day he was seen leading his men into the attack and on several occasions his speech and guidance saved those under his command from ambush and probable annihilation.
>
> At the end of the day when the objective had been successfully reached, this officer went among his men and thanked them for their bravery and endurance. He spoke, and was spoken to in a perfectly natural way. It was only later the same night when the men were told that their commanding officer had been killed early that morning that he ceased to be visible to them and even then there were many who could not be convinced that their leader had 'gone west'. This experience I can vouch for personally as I was there, and I know of others of a similar kind.[17]

Compare the last sentence of that quotation 'This experience I can vouch for personally as I was there, and I know of others of a similar kind', to the penultimate verse in Saint John's gospel, 'This is the disciple who is bearing witness to these things, and who has written these things; and we know that his testimony is true.' (John 21:24).

17. Published by Neville Spearman (1960)

Both writers are claiming to be witnesses of very similar events, the difference lies not in the quality of the post-mortem experiences, but in the cultural conditioning of those who experienced the events.

Jesus' life, teaching, death and post-mortem appearances were set in a particular religious context. There was an expectation, certainly amongst Jesus and his followers, that God was about to intervene in history and bring the world as they knew it to an end. It was expected that the Messiah would come, the Anointed One, who would dramatically redeem the Jewish nation from their bondage (at that time under the Roman empire).

It is not difficult to see how an event such as is described by Tudor Pole above, would be interpreted in First Century Palestine instead of Twentieth Century Palestine. Religious significance would be poured into it in a way that did not happen during World War II. It is easy to see how the Church, in the years which followed the post-mortem appearances of Jesus, looked back through the scriptures to find 'proofs' for their experience from within their own religious culture.

From dogmas such as the immaculate conception of Mary, which followed much later in the Church's history, one can see a retrospective thought process in action. It is not events in themselves which cause doctrine and dogma to be formulated, but rather that particular expectations and perceptions colour events. (We see the world not as it is, but as we are).

To take a modern example: At the end of the Second World War, the atrocities which had been perpetrated upon the Jewish people became evident. There are survivors from the death camps, witnesses from the liberating troops, film footage and still photographs, physical remains (some preserved) of the camps and documented evidence from the Nazis own files. Yet despite all this, there are some people who refuse to believe it. They say that the holocaust never happened, and wish to re-write history to suit their own prejudices. They hear only what they want to hear and see only what they want to see. Their beliefs create the 'facts', rather than the facts creating their beliefs.

Now I am not saying that there was any sinister intent on behalf of the early Church, nor (on the whole) by later churchmen, but their religious beliefs and expectations clearly influenced the facts of Jesus' life as we have received them.

Without the interpretation which the Church subsequently placed upon the resurrection appearances, we can understand the resurrection of Jesus as the appearance of a fully integrated human being after his physical death. Seen in this way, the resurrection accounts become a symbol for the end of our own human journey, possible for every human being, rather than the unique event of a God become man in whom we have to believe to achieve the same end.

The resurrection accounts understood thus, become a symbol of universal hope for the continuance of human existence, rather than the grounds for exclusive claims by a single religion. The Christian explanation of the resurrection 'event' is understandable given the historic conditions in which it took place, and a legitimate interpretation for those who find it so.

But, as I hope I have demonstrated, it is not the only interpretation valid for the Twentieth Century.

Whatever did or did not happen on that first Easter day is something that will have to remain a mystery to us, we simply cannot know. But the importance of the death and resurrection of Jesus go far beyond any historical investigations or doctrinal discussions; they represent for us the very nature of human growth and development. The truth of death and resurrection is found, not in scriptural texts, but within the psyche of humanity.

At a very basic and natural level one can be in touch with this truth through the progressive seasons of the year. In nature the process of birth, death and birth again, happens before our eyes,

159

even if we only have a window box in the middle of a concrete city. Jesus often used analogies from nature in his parables and teaching;

A sower went out to sow... Unless a seed falls into the ground and dies it remains a single grain, but if it dies it bears much fruit... Look at the flowers of the fields... The kingdom of heaven is like a grain of mustard seed...

The human psyche is reflected in the physical and organic nature of the world in which we live. To realise this, and become in tune with it, enables us to mature into full humanity; to become integrated personalities living to capacity.

Unlike other events in the life of Jesus, death and resurrection is not equated with any particular life stage, but is rather, the process which encompasses the whole of our human development. Birth is not possible without death.

For a baby to be born the individual ovum and sperm 'die' to themselves in order to create the foetus.

For the baby to be born it has to 'die' to its own cosy environment of the womb and be pushed out into an alien world (perhaps the most traumatic experience any of us ever have).

For the baby to become an infant, it has to 'die' to its need for milk alone and be born into the world of 'solids'.

The physical process goes on and on.

As an organism we are constantly changing; developing - consolidating - decaying. Being human involves the death and re-birth of our body cells. Only when life stops does this process cease. We can do little to alter or change this natural rhythm.

Exercise, diet, environmental conditions, stress levels - all these will affect to some degree the physical process, but, on the whole it is as relentless in us as it is in nature. The seasons come and the seasons go, and so do we.

Yet if this all sounds rather pessimistic, it is not. Being realistic about our physical condition enables us more acutely to be aware of our spiritual or psychological condition. We may be able to do little or nothing about our physiology (medical interventions excepted), but we can do a great deal about our psyche. An acceptance of death and resurrection as a necessary and inevitable process in our physical life, can lead us into a creative way of living which embraces the same process on the spiritual and psychological level. The world of science uses the very process of death and resurrection in order to advance. Theses are put forward to explain certain phenomena, in the absence of a better explanation they hold sway until, in the light of a better thesis, they are replaced.

Only by this continual process is scientific advancement made. That which was held as 'truth' has to die when a more substantial explanation takes its place. This may be a painful process for an individual scientist or for a scientific community, but in the pursuit of knowledge, death and resurrection, thesis and antithesis go hand in hand.

Accepting death as a way of advancement - I am speaking spiritually and psychologically here - is the key to creative and full living, to living the life of resurrection in the here and now. Death does not cease to be painful, the death of long held ideas, of ways of living, patterns of behaviour, relationship expectations, sexual stereotypes and religious beliefs; to change any of these things is a real psychological death, and the grief process might be profound.

Yet to avoid change, to remain fossilised in the way in which we encounter and react with the world is equally, if not more death-dealing. It is death-dealing for the individual concerned because life becomes limited, vision is narrowed and opportunities missed or resisted. It is also death-dealing for those with whom the individual has to live and work. People who become set in their ways and thoughts, who avoid the pain of death, also avoid the growth and stimulation of resurrection. Such people not only stunt their own growth, but also prevent or frustrate the growth of others by their fear-driven need to maintain the homeostasis (same state) in their lives.

Yet if we reflect for just a moment upon both our own physical condition, and upon the world of nature, we will see that homeostasis is an unnatural condition. To be alive is to change.

If death and resurrection remain nothing more than a belief about a First Century man, we consign to the past the very process which gives us life. As a spiritual director and counsellor I see my main objective as one of enabling others to enter into the process of death and resurrection for themselves. It is about being alongside people as they struggle to liberate themselves from perceptions and attitudes which limit them as people and prevent them from moving towards the goal of authentic living. Often the going is hard, tears are not infrequent and resistance can be fierce, yet we struggle on together because the alternative is worse, an inauthentic life lived under the domination of the past.

For me, as for those with whom I share the spiritual journey, there is always another death to face, the journey does not come to an end in this life, whatever the next may or may not bring. I have often thought of the spiritual journey being a bit like hill-walking.

Sometimes it is cold and miserable, sometimes the fog comes down and visibility all but disappears. There are times when wet through and chilled to the bone, I want nothing more than to be in the warmth of the pub back in the valley. Yet there are those moments of clarity. Moments when the view opens up before me and the spectacle is breath-taking. At those times I know that staying in the pub is really not an option, for no way can it compare with the beauty and vision, the exhilaration and sense of achievement that reaching the top can bring.

But of course, as any hill walker will know, there is always another top, or, if the landscape or seascape is different, another horizon to discover; and the journey goes on.

Whilst I was a Franciscan brother, part of my novitiate was to spend a number of months at the one house in the order which was a monastery rather than a friary, that is, the life was lived mostly

162

within the monastery walls with a good deal of silence.

Immediately prior to this I had been assistant to the Minister Provincial, which meant a great deal of travelling around the various friaries, as well as other external engagements. The change was profound. From an active and high profile life I became the 'least of the brethren' doing everyone's washing in the laundry, and not much liking the change.

During my time in this monastery, where much time is given over to prayer and silence, God went. For me God simply ceased to be, not absent, but non-existent. In the 'power-house of prayer' all that I was left with was a black hole where God had once been. The pain was intense. I wept, I cursed and I went through the motions of the daily routine in dark despair. God had, for me, died; and with God, went my whole reason for being both where I was, and who I was.

This period of utter blackness lasted about two months, (it seemed like two years) but then, out of this very real experience of death, came the resurrection. It is hard for me to put the experience into words. The God in whom I believed up to that point has remained dead, I am more agnostic now about most things than I ever was before, and yet now I know. I do not know about God, but I know deep within my being that there is a dimension to life which has the quality of eternity - that the divine dwells in the very centre of my own being. I felt, and feel resurrected from the tomb of dogmatic belief into the 'liberty of the sons of God'.

For me this was, and remains today a profoundly human experience which I believe is open to all who seek a spiritual way of living.

In holding the death and resurrection of Jesus as central, the Christian Church is holding onto a truth which has significance for the whole of humanity. This significance though is not to do with religious belief, but is the revelation in Jesus of the most profound and universal laws of the universe. The process of death and resurrection is built into the human psyche as a means of achieving the fullness of the human condition.

It is, to use the words of C.S. Lewis from *The Lion, the Witch and the Wardrobe*, "the deep magic from before the dawn of time".

One can call the result of such a process 'the kingdom of God' or, in Jungian terms 'individuation' or from Eastern traditions 'enlightenment'. The name we give it is only relevant insofar as it enables or prevents people from entering into the process for themselves. The process of 'becoming' through death and resurrection is a profoundly human process. In Jesus the Church has a magnificent icon to enable and encourage followers on the journey to wholeness; it must realise however that the truth which he embodies is for all, regardless of their religious affiliation.

Do not therefore be afraid of the pain which death brings, for in its wake comes a newness and quality of life which can truly be called resurrection.

In his little book *The Prophet* Kahlil Gibran writes: "Your pain is the breaking of the shell that encloses your understanding."

Breaking the shell (or the mould) is a radical process. The spiritual life challenges both our own personal norms and often the norms of our society. Do not set out on the path of death and resurrection if you want a quiet life; you will be called to be as radical today as Jesus was in his time. But in dying you will live, and eternity will break in upon you, and you will never be the same again.

CHAPTER 20
Ascension - Being who I'm meant to be

Children can often give us amusing, but nevertheless quite penetrating insights into taking biblical texts too literally.

A mother was mystified when listening to her children talking. The older child, who was about six years old, was telling the younger one all about God. It appeared from this conversation that God was left handed, in fact not only was God left handed, but he only used his left hand. When the child was questioned about this, the answer was quite straight forward, for it says in Mark 16:19, "So then after the Lord had spoken unto them, he was received up into heaven, and sat on the right hand of God." (King James version). And in the Book of Common Prayer, the Creed states; "...And ascended into heaven, And sitteth on the right hand of the Father."

This obviously forced God into left handedness from that time onwards!

The story of the ascension of Jesus comes to us via the author of 'Luke' and 'The Acts of the apostles'. Matthew and John are silent on the subject, and, as we have seen from above, the Gospel of Mark gives us very little to go on, and what is there, is thought to be a later addition to the original text.

The Gospel of Luke says:

While he was blessing them, he withdrew from them and was carried up into heaven.[18]

Yet not all of the early texts include "and was carried up into heaven", so there is little here to go on in Luke's Gospel to sustain a doctrine of Jesus' ascension 'into heaven'.

The fullest text that we have comes from 'The Acts of the Apostles'. We read:

18. Luke 24:51

165

When he had said this, as they were watching, he was lifted up, and a cloud took him out of their sight. While he was going and they were gazing up toward heaven, suddenly two men in white robes stood by them. They said, "Men of Galilee, why do you stand looking up toward heaven? This Jesus, who has been taken up from you into heaven, will come in the same way as you saw him go into heaven".[19]

We can laugh at the story of the child, with Jesus 'sitting on God's right hand' for evermore, yet that is only one step away from what the Church has managed to construct from some very meagre texts. Still the Church conveys the idea that the ascension is about the bodily vertical take-off of Jesus, a sort of jet-propelled figure disappearing into the stratosphere. Whatever did or did not actually happen, I feel sure about one thing; the ascension is not about having to believe in rocketless aeronautics. Chapels dedicated to the ascension with a pair of plaster feet sticking out from a plaster cloud in the ceiling may have been a helpful 'visual aid' in times past, but it does nothing for me (except raise a smile) as we approach the third millennium AD.

So what are we to make of the ascension? And what relevance does it have for us today?

Like most of the other 'events' in the life of Jesus, I remain agnostic about just how much is based on some historical happening, and how much is mythological interpretation given to the life of Jesus by the early Church.

If as we saw in the previous chapter, the resurrection appearances of Jesus were not unlike, although perhaps qualitatively different, from the appearances described by Tudor Pole, then some sort of dematerialisation would seem a possible outcome. But this is still a long way off bodily ascension.

If it were a mythological interpretation then we can see how

19. Acts 1:9-11

166

the language of ascension would be used. In a time when 'heaven' was thought to be another 'place', quite literally above the sky, and that this was where God 'dwelt', then 'going up' was another way of saying that Jesus was now in a closer relationship with God. Ascension represents a completion, a 'going home', an 'at-one-ment'. It is at this point that we can identify with the story and make it our own.

Whatever we believe did or did not really happen to Jesus, the ascension speaks to us of our own completion of the journey; it is the goal to which our humanity is directed, a wholeness of being which, for those who want to use such language, may be called divine.

As a model for our own humanity, the ascension of Jesus points to our own total integration; of being at-one both with ourselves, and with the world in which we live. Carl Jung used the word 'individuation' to describe the same process, or rather the end point of the process of becoming who we really are. In this life it seems to me that it is likely that few, if any people achieve this full state of integration or individuation. There are so many possibilities for each individual, so much potential which probably never gets the opportunity to be fulfilled, that full integration remains a possibility rather than a probability for us in this life.

In his book *Jungian Dream Interpretations*, James Hall puts it this way:

> Individuation... refers to the process in which a person in actual life consciously attempts to understand and develop the innate individual potentialities of his or her own psyche. Because the archetypal possibilities are so vast, any particular individuation process inevitably must fail to achieve all that is innately possible. The important factor, therefore is not the amount of achievement, *but whether the personality*

167

is being true to its own deep potentialities rather than simply following egocentric and narcissistic tendencies or identifying with collective cultural roles.[20]

Being true to our own deepest potential is the very nature of the spiritual journey; it is about discovering, and then living out our true self. This will involve many acts of death and resurrection. It will mean going beyond the satisfaction of the 'little me' who would like instant gratification, to the deeper Self which, cojectively, connects with the deepest Self in others, and with the very Being of the universe in which we live. When we start to transcend our own individual and neurotic selves, then we begin to experience wholeness and healing within our personalities.

In his Tavistock Lectures, Jung writes about the healing process:

> It is an individuation process, an identification with the totality of the personality, with the self. In Christian symbolism the totality is Christ, and the healing process consists of the 'Imitatio Christi'.[21]

Jung is saying here that healing comes through the imitation of Christ, yet, the most profound moments of Christ's life, as we have received them through the gospels, cannot be imitated by us if they are taken literally and historically. We can only imitate Christ if we see his whole life as a profound myth, a model or paradigm for our own humanity. To truly imitate Christ is not to try and be like he was, for he was a particular person in a given historical and cultural setting.

To imitate Christ in this way is a mistake which Christians have made throughout the ages. It is a mistake for two reasons. Firstly it makes the person of Jesus exclusive rather than inclusive;

20. Inner City Books, Toronto, (1983) (My Italics)
21. Analytical Psychology, Routledge & Keegan Paul, London (1986)

but secondly and more importantly, it produces in us inauthentic living. To imitate Christ in his actions, teaching, behaviour and so forth, is to negate who we really are by copying someone else. This is nothing more than hero-worship, and will certainly not lead us on our own journey of integration and wholeness.

When I was a boy my hero was Steve Reeves. He was one-time Mr. Universe who became a film actor in epic tales of strength and 'derring-dos'. I can still conjure-up some pictures in my mind. Two teams of horses, one strapped to either of his arms. Whipped to go in opposite directions they were meant to tear him apart. He of course was too strong for them and won the day. Steve Reeves was my hero because he was everything I was not.

When I 'rode' one of the living room chairs, (which became a chariot) I was no longer a weedy little boy picked on by larger boys at school, I was the strongest man in the world, ready to take on all comers.

Hero worship, whether it is the childish dreams of a small boy for a super hero taken on into adult life, or the devout imitation of a religious follower of Christ is equally neurotic. It is about being less than we really are by placing another person where our truest self ought to be.

To truly follow Christ is in no way to copy him, but to recognise that he lived his life as a fully authenticated human being. Only by imitating this aspect will we be going down the road of true spirituality, of integration and individuation. Only by being truly and fully ourselves can we be true to the spirit of Christ. Jesus presents us, not with a mould into which we have to try and fit, but with an example of human potential lived out to the full.

The ascension of Christ represents for us that stage of integration which is our destiny as human beings. Because integration is a process, and because it requires constant commitment to a particular way of being and becoming, it will normally be equated with the last stage of our lives - old age. Yet there is nothing automatic about ascension/integration.

By the time that we have reached old age we have had the opportunity to integrate ourselves with all of life's experiences. It can be a time of reflection, a time when competition is no longer important, or of less importance, and when honesty, both with oneself and with others, becomes more of a possibility. However, it is clear that in fact, age is not the determining factor in achieving an integrated personality. If I have set my life on a course of spiritual growth, cojective values and individuation, then by the time I reach old age, there is a good chance that I will have (nearly) achieved it.

If, on the other hand, the maintenance of neurotic defences and the protection of my ego has become a way of life, then no matter how long I may live, I am unlikely to achieve or even approach being a fully integrated person. Old age therefore does not, of necessity, bring with it integration and wholeness of life; what long life offers is the opportunity. How we use that opportunity is up to us.

Likewise, a short life does not rule out the possibility of achieving an integrated life, Jesus was, after all, only about 33 years old when he died, but few of us give ourselves to the spiritual journey as he did, so we must hope for sufficient time to bring our lives to the state of completeness which is possible.

The ascension of Christ then has nothing to do with supernatural aeronautics, the peculiar end to an equally peculiar man. No, ascension is the myth which represents the end of our own journey. The Atonement is not a doctrine in which we have to believe, but rather at-one-ment is the goal for our own lives, achievable by us because, in Christ, we see the possibilities of what a fully human life can be like.

Again, like the other 'events' in the life of Jesus, if you choose to take a more literalistic view of the ascension than I do, if plaster feet in plaster clouds symbolise something of great importance to you, well and good; your view is as valid as mine. What is important is that it is your view, and not something second-hand which you feel you somehow have to believe.

Whether you hold a literalist view of the ascension, or an agnostic approach to the event itself, and a mythological interpretation of its meaning, is of no great importance. One thing is vital though, to our spiritual life and therefore to our humanity. We must allow the 'event' of the ascension to be a living fact in our own lives. Only when the ascension becomes more than an intellectual exercise or a statement of belief will it affect who we are. It is about Being. Being who we are meant to be, the end of our spiritual journey; and unless we have a goal to look forward to, the journey is hardly worth starting in the first place.

CHAPTER 21

The Pearl of Great Price

The theme running through this book has been one of spiritual journeying. It has taken us into different places which, on the surface would seem as far removed from one another as Africa is from the Antarctic. Developmental psychology has been rubbing shoulders with children's fairy stories, theology with popular culture, sex with prayer, and belief with disbelief.

Yet this is how it should be, for our journey is about finding our own authentic selves, becoming true to our deepest nature, and learning to live in ways which are truly fulfilling. Our search therefore is bound to take us into, and sometimes, out of again, all the experiences which belong to our human condition. We have our being in and through our bodies, our humanity is enfleshed, and so it is through this world that we learn to discover our truest and deepest selves. Yet this does mean accepting all that we experience.

Much of what constitutes human living today is a shallow imitation of the real thing. It may give passing pleasure or an illusion of happiness, but it has no depth, nor any ability to fill the deepest desires of our human condition. Very many people, if they are being honest with themselves, know this to be true. There is a hollowness in their lives which craves more and more to be filled, and the more it is filled with the distractions of wealth, power and possessions, or religion, piety and false humility, greater becomes the void. The tragic cycle continues until people really come to equate themselves with these exterior distractions; the authentic self is lost under the accumulation of acquired status.

In his short parable, Jesus sums up this condition.

"Again, the kingdom of heaven is like a merchant in

search of fine pearls; on finding one pearl of great value, he went and sold all that he had and bought it.[22]

For a very long time I did not see what was really being said in this story. I equated the "kingdom of heaven" with something religious, and the "selling all that he had" in a literal and materialistic way. Nothing could be further from the truth.

The 'pearl of great price' is our own authentic being; it is who we have it in us to really be, and to actually be that person. It has nothing to do with being religious in itself. Although that may be a route we choose to take, it is not a necessary route.

The route is one of spirituality as I have tried to define in these pages. It is a human process which places at its centre that spirit which is cojectively experienced by all people. It is the spirit which looks for the good in others, it is the spirit which expresses itself in acts of love and kindness, tolerance and understanding. It is the spirit which refuses to be 'palmed off' with shoddy imitations and glitzy counterfeits of the real thing.

In the parable, the merchant had to sell all that he had in order to obtain this one pearl of great price; this is no less true for us. But the cost is much higher than just selling our material wealth, however much or little that is. The cost involved is a 'selling', a letting go of our old self, the persona which we have carefully cultivated over the course of our lives.

Many find the cost too high. Although in the depths of their hearts they know that life is far from satisfactory, despite perhaps having great material power and wealth (or maybe because of it), they cannot face changing what has been constructed over a long period of time. The pain of unsatisfactory living seems less frightening than the thought of change.

To live authentically as the human being that we most truly are, is the pearl of great price. It is a profoundly human goal which can be sought after through any religion or none.

22. Matthew 13:45

Religion can be, and often is, detrimental to the process because it denies the authority of the individual in favour of obedience to doctrines and dogmas, which can have no authority unless they speak to the heart of the individual.

As Leslie Weatherhead said in his book *The Christian Agnostic*, "the words 'ought' and 'believe' cannot go together." A belief which is no more than an acceptance of a given doctrine, or of the social norms of our particular society, is no belief at all. We prostitute our truest selves to our religion or social set in order to belong, in order to feel accepted. Yet it is not our true self which is accepted, it is a persona, the mask which we have carefully built up. On the outside we are one of the in-group, on the inside we feel lonely, often desperate, knowing that, "If only they knew who I really was" or "If only they knew what I really believed, they wouldn't like me at all."

The message of the spiritual journey is that we can be our true selves, but it will be at the cost of our persona.

This is the second attempt to write the concluding chapter. In the first draft I said that my book was an offering which was not out to convert anybody. I said that if you, the reader, did not like it, never mind, cast is aside.

After Ruth read it she said I was being dishonest, that I did want to convert people, and that I would be sorry if people did just dismiss what I said; which of course is true. I suppose what I hope this book might do is to enable change. I do not want to convert anyone in the sense that my 'doctrine' should not be adhered to any more than any other 'doctrine', religious or secular.

If you 'believe' anything written in these pages, and if that belief goes on to affect your life, let it be because it resonates within you, because it 'connects' with that which is most authentic in your own life. In that sense it is an offering, for if it does not resonate within you, if something of my truth does not connect with something of your truth, then it should be laid aside. Spiritual truths can never

175

be forced upon anybody, only offered. And the one who does the offering (of his or her own truth) does so in a certain style, with a particular use of language and from a particular psychological, historical and cultural perspective, and this will not suit everybody.

My greatest hope is that, if in some small way this book can enable a cojective view of spirituality, a lessening of barriers between religious and non-religious, and between religions of different understandings, it will have served its purpose. If in these pages you have found something which enables you, helps you towards authentic living, releases you from imposed 'doctrines' of whatever type, my fumbling efforts will have been worth-while.

Nothing written in these pages is done with a sense of finality or objectivity. For me there always needs to be an element of the provisional, a sense that tomorrow, next week, next year will bring new insights, new ways of understanding myself and the world in which I am privileged to live. It is of course an unsettling place to be - the land of the provisional - yet it is also exciting, stimulating and fun.

To start on the spiritual journey needs, to begin with, only small acts, small changes in our perception, which will begin to affect who we are. For spirituality is chiefly about changing ourselves, finding our own 'pearl of great price'. I am at heart, optimistic about humanity and about the world.

Although we live in times when there seems to be unequalled violence and upset around us, (or is it that it is just more available to us today?) I believe that at the heart of women and men lies a deep goodness which is possible for all of us to contact. We do not have to be victims; victims of our past, victims of other individuals, victims of society. No matter how deplorable our situation (unless our mental capacity is too damaged to function normally), we can make choices which can improve both our lot, and the lot of those around us.

Even small choices which seem insignificant can begin to effect a change, the end of which we may never know. Small acts of kindness like smiling and saying 'thank you' to the ticket collector or newspaper vendor can make all the difference, to us, if not to them.

When I was a Franciscan brother I did a lot of hitch-hiking all over Britain. Needless to say, only one in several hundred cars ever stopped to pick me up. This was sometimes quite depressing, especially when the weather was cold and wet, but one piece of advice kept me in good fettle, it was this: 'Whenever a car passes you, give the driver a blessing'. The drivers in this case knew nothing of my blessing, so its effect on them can hardly be contemplated, but the effect on me was noticeable. It somehow kept me operating at a level which went far deeper than the discomfort of a wet roadside stop. It enabled me to transcend my 'outer self' and find a peace which the situation did not warrant. When we 'look to the good', give a blessing and not a curse, and take the time to connect with people at a human and humane level, we begin to change our own inner world, and also begin to affect the world in which we live for the better.

These little acts and thoughts may seem like no more than spitting in the ocean, but repeated enough times by individuals it will transform their lives for the better; repeated enough times by millions of people and the world could be changed!

To start out on, and engage in the spiritual journey is to want to change myself for the better as a human being. It is to want to have a positive effect on the world in which we live. It is to recognise and respect the uniqueness of each individual's path, so that we never deny another person's truth. Certainly we can say that their truth is not our truth, but we must be very cautious in saying that our truth ought to be their truth.

In his book on Transactional Analysis, Thomas Harris wrote this:

It takes only one generation for a good thing to become a bad thing, for an inference about an experience to become a dogma.

Dogma is the enemy of truth and the enemy of persons. Dogma says 'Do not think! be less than a person.' The ideas enshrined in dogma may include good and wise ideas, but the dogma is bad in itself because it is accepted as good without examination.[23]

We must avoid dogma in both institutions and ourselves (he says dogmatically) because it does not allow for the authentic expression of the individual to find what is true for them. Jesus never tried to 'convert' anyone into a belief system or code of laws, rather he loved them for who they were and where they were. In doing this he enabled them to respond from the depths of their own, albeit sometimes very damaged, beings, and to begin the process of becoming whole and integrated.

What was good enough for a man like Jesus (without any Christian preconceptions about his nature) is good enough for me. At the end of the day I believe we are called to love. Loving is no easy task, it takes a great deal of hard work, perseverance, tolerance and discipline. It demands of us to really get to know ourselves, our deepest motivations, the parts which even certain lagers cannot reach. It also demands that we remain agnostic about a good many things.

If we are religious, then we need to acknowledge that our particular religion will reflect something of the truth, but certainly not all of it, and that which it does reflect may, over the years have become tarnished and less than perfect. If we are not religious, we need to acknowledge that there is perhaps hidden wisdom within religion which reflects our human struggle for integration and wholeness.

To dismiss religion too readily is to assess it at a level which probably owes more to a kindergarten understanding, than to a

23. I'm OK - You're OK, Pan Books, London (1973)

serious study of the literature or practice of any given religion. I grow more and more agnostic as the years go by, yet this somehow seems to be far more comfortable with my humanity. I am beginning to see that knowing about, being sure of any *thing* does not really matter at all, even if that thing is my religious belief. What matters, what really counts is that I learn to be fully me, a person who can relate to other persons at the deepest levels of our being. So often it has been my experience that religion actually prevents this person to person interaction. It has got in the way because beliefs have been more important than my brother or sister with whom I have been talking.

The spiritual path may go under many different names or none, but what is common is a sense of purpose, a discipline which is not satisfied with inauthentic living, and a concern for our fellow creatures - at all levels of the created order.

In his wonderful little modern myth *Jonathan Livingston Seagull*, Richard Bach put his finger on the pulse of spirituality. Jonathan has just 'died', and is learning on a new plane of being with the Elder gull, Chiang...

> "We can start working with time if you wish," Chiang said, "till you can fly the past and the future. And then you will be ready to begin the most difficult, the most powerful, the most fun of all. You will be ready to begin to fly up and know the meaning of kindness and of love."

Those two words, kindness and love, have been sentimentalised and devalued in our modern world, but both things require a strength of will and a steadfastness of purpose unmatched by any materialistic discipline known to humanity.

Perhaps that is why religion is such a popular alternative, because like a travel programme on the television, it offers the prospect of the journey without ever leaving your seat (pew).

The spiritual journey is the way of becoming fully who we have it in us to be; it is a way of life which brings the highest degree of satisfaction for the individual, and the greatest hope for the future of our planet. Now is the time to discard the clutter which binds us to limited visions, and separates one human being from another. Let go of your security blanket and throw your caution to the wind of the spirit. The adventure is just beginning, the journey is yours, and the goal is integration and wholeness of being.

Saint Augustine said, "Love and then what you will, do." Let this be your motto for the spiritual journey; it will undoubtedly lead you into some pretty tight spots where religion or materialism seem like great alternatives. But don't despair, look for someone who is even deeper in the mire than yourself and help to pull him out. That will help to put both of you back on the road.

So here we are at the end of the book. I feel that the whole thing could really be summed up by saying "be loving and practice kindness." This is the essence of the spiritual life, it is the essence of being truly human. We need make it no more complicated than this, in doing so we only erect walls to separate. Let your love build bridges, and your acts of kindness be the means by which you communicate with your fellow travellers, for nothing makes life so worth living as the bond which forms between people on the road.

An old Celtic blessing would seem a fitting way to wish you a good journey.

> May the road rise up to meet you,
> May the wind be always at your back,
> May the sun shine warm upon your face,
> May the rain fall softly upon your fields
> > until we meet again,
> May God hold you in the hollow of his hand.